HOW AM I WIRED?

CHANGE BEGINS WITH

UNDERSTANDING WHY

I AM THE WAY I AM

SECOND EDITION

Eve J. Day M.A.C.C. &

David Alan Greene Ph.D.

ii

GRACEWORD PUBLISHING

iv

To our friends and family who are themselves
creations of the Magnificent Creator

Table of Contents

1 Introduction 1
2 Understanding What Happened . . . 11
3 Created In His Image 21
4 What Is The Temperament? 33
5 Temperament Overview 41
6 Introducing The Choleric 51
7 An Example Of The Choleric 61
8 Introducing The Melancholic 71
9 An Example Of The Melancholic . . . 79
10 Introducing The Phlegmatic 85
11 An Example Of The Phlegmatic 93
12 Introducing The Sanguine 97
13 An Example Of The Sanguine 103
14 Introducing The Supine 109
15 An Example Of The Supine 115
16 One Of A Kind 121
17 Temperament Therapy 129
Resource 133
Other GraceWord Publications 135
About The Authors 137

1

Introduction

Many people feel there is something wrong with them. In all cases, they would be right. We cannot think of one person we have ever met that is perfect and that, of course, includes us. You might think that this is a somewhat controversial or bold statement to make at the very beginning. However, we should dispel any misconception that this book or, for that matter, anything will ever make someone perfect. Why? The reason is there is something wrong with all of us.

We opened the book with that statement because many people are under the impression that if they could just fix this or that, then they would be perfect and all of their problems would go away. Unfortunately, that is not life. Having such an expectation will only lead to disappointment because the expected outcome is impossible. Life is ongoing. It presents us with a constant source of challenges to which we must adapt. How we adapt to those challenges is how this book can help you.

There is good news. Here is an interesting question to consider: *What if you knew how you were wired?* Before we get to the purpose of this book, we must first present you with an important belief. It will be presented in a way that you can think about it. We will get into greater detail as we move through the book.

The belief is that we are all created and, as such, we each received a unique set of temperament components which will be with us throughout our life. It makes us who we are, how we feel, and how we react. Understanding these unique components will not only help us to understand ourselves but also understand others.

It is possible to change by learning how to adapt. You will not become someone else. Our book presents this information based upon the idea that you are who you are because you were *fearfully and wonderfully made.* You were designed. You were not randomly amalgamated into who you are. You were designed! To those reading this book who are Evolutionists, you may want to stop here. The remainder of the book is built upon the idea that we were created and, therefore, we can have a relationship with the Creator.

Some of the ideas presented in this book will differ from those which you have learned over the years. Many traditional or secular methods will differ because of the basic premise stated above. Reconsidering our beliefs allows us to change them or keep what we believe. Questioning what we believe may feel frightening but, in the end, it strengthens us. We either change what we accept as truth or we become more confident in our current beliefs. We will start by examining the idea contained in the words *fearfully and wonderfully made*. Then we can decide which of two options we will choose. Please allow us to explain.

Whether we call it our *philosophy of life* or our *life view*, we must recognize that this is how we interpret life as a whole. Everything must fall into our system of interpretation. If there are things which seem contrary to our existing system, we must either reject it or reconcile it. In the current situation under discussion, the choice is whether we believe in *intelligent design* or *evolution of the species*. It is neither the purpose of this book to argue either in favor of or against either of these two positions. To do so would take up too much space and detract us from our purpose. However, choosing one over the other will change your entire perspective because you are changing your entire belief system. We have the freedom to make that decision and to change. Either way, it has no effect on truth itself.

The title of this book is *How Am I Wired.* It was named so because the very title suggests there is an Electrician. That would be the Someone Who did the wiring. Here is an illustration. There are people who love watches. They admire them for their beauty but also for the marvelous artistic detail as well as the mechanical precision. To behold a beautiful timepiece in your hand and believe that it somehow came together by chance or evolved from nothing, would be ridiculous. Therefore, going forward, the presented information will be based upon the belief we were created. We were wired by the Creator's hand.

Not only were we wired, but we were wired as someone totally unique from all others. Evolutionists hold that we are random products of evolution. We are indistinct from each other and, therefore, are interchangeable units of human existence. On the other hand, Creationists hold that we were individually created to be unique and valued creations. We understand this may upset some people. Let us politely say to them, this book is not for you.

When we speak of *wiring,* we are referring to how someone functions as an individual both mentally and emotionally. It is simply an illustration to explain how we work internally. You may have heard the saying *That's just how he's wired* as an explanation as to why someone does something. It means that this is how he operates–almost automatically. It could be an inherent tendency, an instinctive reaction, or auto-response we feel we are almost compelled to do. It is instinctive. This, friends, is the focus of this book. We will look at what is the cause of these tendencies. Where do they come from and, perhaps most importantly, can we change or adapt them?

Personal Note from David Greene:

> Philosophers, scientists, theologians, and teachers have spent years trying to come to an understanding of why people act the way they do. Speaking from personal experience, as when raising my three children, I observed that each of them was totally unique in the way they interacted with the world and with each other. Each thought differently as they processed information and interacted with other people. I had found a book in our

church's library by Tim LaHaye. You may know him as the author of the popular *Left Behind* series. This book was titled *Spirit-Controlled Temperament* and was originally written in 1966. I believe it was one of the first books to present the theory of individual *temperaments*. For thirty-five years this concept helped me in my profession as an independent insurance agent. Recognizing that people are different and adapting to their *temperament* gave me a more effective way to communicate. It helped me to recognize particular temperaments and adapt my presentation to their unique needs.

You may have heard people referring to someone as a Type-A or Type-B personality. The former type meant a task-oriented person, sometimes called "the hunter." The latter was a people-oriented person, sometimes called "the gatherer." This "hunter-gatherer" division would be similar to the "leader-follower." Neither help us to understand the divergent complexities, only that there are differences. Note that the word they used above was *personality*.

Many counselors deal with the *personality* of their client and try to understand how it developed. We will explain this from a different perspective. The terms *personality* and *temperament*, as we define them, are completely different from each other. For our purpose going forward, we will need to see *temperament* and *personality* as being distinctively different in their meaning.

Personal Note from David Greene:

> The model presented by Tim LaHaye in his book *Spirit-Controlled Temperament* was based upon a model of four temperaments: melancholic, choleric, sanguine, and phlegmatic. After I completed my theological degrees at seminary, I decided to pursue additional studies which would help me in my ability to explain and teach the Bible to a diverse group of people. I was blessed with the opportunity to meet Drs. Richard and Phyllis Arno. They devoted much of their lives to studying, understanding, and developing the temperament model in greater detail.

Drs. Richard and Phyllis Arno expanded LaHaye's model to include a fifth temperament called the Supine. Later in the book, we will examine and discuss all five in greater detail. They also taught that each individual has three areas in which these five temperaments would apply. After years of combined clinical study, we both have great confidence in the accuracy of temperament assessments endorsed by the National Christian Counselors Association.

These temperament assessments determine the predominant temperament composition which each individual has. It identifies three specific areas: *Inclusion*, *Control*, and *Affection*. Each of these will be explained in greater detail later in this book.

We need to pause for a moment. If we limit each of the five temperaments to these three components, then there would be a potential outcome of fifteen unique combinations. That would make each person somewhat unique. However, Drs. Arno's research has determined that the five temperaments can be subdivided further into something similar to a range on an X-Y graph. They created this grid-like report of nine columns and nine rows for each temperament. That would increase the outcome for each temperament to eighty-one possibilities. Applying this to each of the three specific areas of *Inclusion*, *Control*, and *Affection*, the possibilities increase exponentially for unique combinations of temperaments.

We are all unique. Each of us was hand-crafted, personally wired or designed by the Creator of the Universe. This is certainly a different approach when compared to that of our colleagues in secular counseling. An intimate relationship between the Creator was intended from the moment of conception. As Christian counselors, we often turn to the Bible to get God's perspective on matters like this. David, King of Israel, was addressing God when he wrote in Psalm 139:13-14:

> 13 For thou hast possessed my reins:
> thou hast covered me in my mother's
> womb.
> 14 I will praise thee; for <u>I am fearfully
> and wonderfully made</u>: marvellous are
> thy works; and that my soul knoweth
> right well.

2

Understand What Happened

We chose the title of this book as a question, *How Am I Wired?* We did this because it presumes that, at the time of our creation, we were inherently wired by the Creator. The way we think and act, the way we are wired, was done before we were born. We will see that our temperament, which we referred to as "wired" in the title, was actually given to each of us at the moment when we were conceived and life began. At that moment we were uniquely made.

With this in mind, we must begin by presupposing the existence of a "system designer" or Creator. This concept of an orderly design with intended purposes or functions is called *Intelligent Design.* We should feel in awe that each of us was hand-crafted by the Creator of the Universe while we were *knitted together* in our mother's womb (*cf.* Ps. 139:13 ESV)."

This makes each of us very special.

In Genesis, we read "So God created man in his own image, in the image of God created he him; male and female created he them" (Gen. 1:27). Without going into great detail as to the theological implications, we can know we were made by God and we were made in His image, or likeness. It was the Creator's intention to have an intimate relationship with His creatures. The Apostle Luke records the genealogy of Jesus Christ beginning with Joseph and going back to Adam where it all began (*cf.* Lk. 3:23-38). In the last verse Adam is called "the son of God" because he was physically created by the hand of God. Adam, created in God's likeness, was the progenitor of the entire human race.

What happened to this intimate relationship? You could say that there was a breakdown in the relationship between God and Adam. Adam rebelled against God. Being the children of Adam, we were all included in Adam's fall. The story of this fall of Adam, specifically, and mankind, in general, was recorded for us in Genesis chapters 1–3. Adam and Eve chose to disobey God's direct command. They had an opportunity to eat the forbidden fruit. They chose to eat of that fruit so that they too would be like God. The result of their disobedience was expulsion from the

Garden of Eden. We read in Genesis 3:22–24:

> 22 And the LORD God said, Behold, the man is become as one of us, to know good and evil: and now, lest he put forth his hand, and take also of the tree of life, and eat, and live for ever: 23 Therefore the LORD God sent him forth from the garden of Eden, to till the ground from whence he was taken. 24 So he drove out the man; and he placed at the east of the garden of Eden Cherubims, and a flaming sword which turned every way, to keep the way of the tree of life.

The consequence of their action was far reaching. You may remember the reference in a traditional Christmas carol "far as the curse is found." The curse referred to in that carol is the pronouncement God made upon Adam and creation itself. We suffer from this curse even today and it will continue until the final restoration. A curse put upon both Adam continues upon all his descendants. Here is the pronouncement of the fateful sentence upon the serpent, the first couple, and their offspring. In Genesis 3:14–19, we read:

> 14 And the LORD God said unto the ser-

pent, Because thou hast done this, thou art cursed above all cattle, and above every beast of the field; upon thy belly shalt thou go, and dust shalt thou eat all the days of thy life: 15 And I will put enmity between thee and the woman, and between thy seed and her seed; it shall bruise thy head, and thou shalt bruise his heel.

16 Unto the woman he said, I will greatly multiply thy sorrow and thy conception; in sorrow thou shalt bring forth children; and thy desire shall be to thy husband, and he shall rule over thee. 17 And unto Adam he said, Because thou hast hearkened unto the voice of thy wife, and hast eaten of the tree, of which I commanded thee, saying, Thou shalt not eat of it: cursed is the ground for thy sake; in sorrow shalt thou eat of it all the days of thy life; 18 Thorns also and thistles shall it bring forth to thee; and thou shalt eat the herb of the field; 19 In the sweat of thy face shalt thou eat bread, till thou return unto the ground; for out of it wast thou taken: for dust thou art, and unto dust shalt thou return.

The curse was the direct result of their own choice–their freewill. They had alienated themselves from God. The former perfect relationship between the couple and the Creator had been damaged. You can see the above proclamation includes a portion that affects us physically, but there is an effect to us spiritually as well. In knowing the difference between good and evil, we each have a natural tendency to choose evil.

After the fall, the remainder of the Old Testament records the history of Adam's descendants. The first murder was one of Adam's sons killing his brother. The results of evil did not take long to manifest itself. You might want to know what this has to do with understanding how you are wired? It has everything to do with it. Let us tie it all together for you.

Remember that, as a descendent of Adam, you are operating in a fallen state. Your natural bent is to fall short of what is right. You might know another word for "falling short" or "missing the mark." Since the fall of Adam and Eve, mankind has been dealing with one thing that had not existed until then. What is that? It is called "sin." Take anything which is perfect and sin can mess it up. The important thing to remember right now is that you were not wired incorrectly. However, how you were wired will affect the tendencies or the ways you will choose to sin in life. Remember two things: first, sin always remains a choice and, second, there are always consequences for sin.

The Greek word for sin, *harmartia*, means "missing the mark." It was a term used in archery. All of us fall short and miss the mark. Paul writes, "For all have sinned, and come short of the glory of God" (Rom. 3:23). Our nature has a bent towards sin. As a result of Adam's fall, something inside us was broken or, perhaps a better illustration, our wiring got frayed. Picture a bolt of lightning striking a building which is a server farm, a warehouse filled with thousands of computers. Sometimes the damage is evident and other times it will manifest itself later. That is an explanation as to why sometimes people choose to do what they do. We read the newspapers, watch the news, or catch up with events by surfing the internet. We are appalled at the things people say and do. We ask ourselves "How could anyone do that?" or "Why would anyone say that?" The Bible uses the word *evil* which is the result of turning away from the Creator and choosing to become our own *god*. Turning towards God and not away from Him is the only solution to this problem.

We continue with our exploration of temperament.

Please keep in mind the concept of sin being rebellion. This is the biblical explanation of why people do bad things. All of us were affected by Adam's fall. The Apostle John writes, "If we say that we have no sin, we deceive ourselves, and the truth is not in us" (1 Jn. 1:8). It is a fact. At times, each of us is subject to the desire to sin. Each person has the power to exercise their freewill to either sin or not. This fact will become more important to understanding ourselves later on. For now, just remember that God created us.

How Am I Wired?

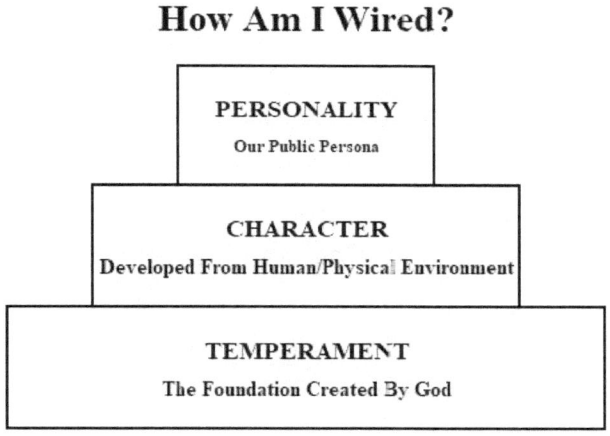

PERSONALITY
Our Public Persona

CHARACTER
Developed From Human/Physical Environment

TEMPERAMENT
The Foundation Created By God

In Temperament Therapy there is something called The Building Blocks as shown in this diagram above. You can see that *temperament* is the foundation which God has created within each of us. Once the foundation is laid, it is unchangeable. It will help to think of a building foundation upon which the entire structure is built.

Although each of us has different life experiences, different physical environments, and social groups with which we interact, the foundation remains the same. The middle block deals with these external influences. This creates our *character* which changes and adapts as we mature and gain more experience. Our character may be influenced by external forces and environments. However, our temperament remains unchanged.

The final component of these building blocks is the *personality*. Sometimes the personality is referred to as *the mask* because is it the part of us we want people to see. We could call it our *public persona*. The word *persona* is defined as "the role that one assumes or displays in public or society; one's public image or personality, as distinguished from the inner self." This is the public perception we want to present and, as such, it may or may not be our true self.

The purpose of this chapter was to dispel the belief that, if God made us the way we are, then He must be the One responsible for why we are the way we are. It is true that God made us. A short study of the book of Genesis will confirm that everything God made pleased Him because it was good. At the finish of creation, God had accomplished His intended purpose. However, the consequences of Adam's sin reach far beyond Adam and Eve individually. It affected all of their direct descendants as well as the physical world in which we live.

We will look at the individual temperaments. When we do, we will examine them from two perspectives. First, we want to consider what was the original intent of each temperament's strengths. Second, we look at each set of weaknesses or tendencies towards sin we have that are inherent with each temperament style. As we work to understand our temperament, we will use the same non-critical, non-judgmental approach used in Temperament Therapy to understand why we are the way we are and why we do the things we do.

3

Created In His Image

Now we are at the core of the matter. Unfolding what the temperament is and its components will be different from traditional psychology in several ways. The word *psychology* comes from Greek. It is a compound word with *psyche* meaning "soul" and *logia* meaning the "knowledge or study." Another word for soul is the mind. Psychology is the study of the mind. If you have been to a counselor, you might recognize some of the comparisons we make below. However, you will find that Temperament Therapy is different.

Much of what is presented here is based upon the findings of Drs. Richard and Phyllis Arno. Their dedication to developing and testing these theories has been the heart of their ministry to help people understand who God created them to be. It is their research which allows us to understand how God wired us and it is the basis of the following information. For their devotion to this cause, we humbly express our abundant gratitude.

Most secular counselors focus their therapy on the client's personality. They attempt to understand the personality by probing and analyzing the client's past. They spend a considerable amount of time asking about the client's history. Somehow, it is as if we came into this world as a blank slate, a concept is called *Tabula Rasa*. They believe that once we are born, we begin writing our experience upon it.

Certainly, our experiences do affect us. Yes, we are a composite of our experiences, but there is something that goes much deeper than this. We hold the view that we are not animals which evolved higher than other species. It is because we were created by intelligent design that the following will make sense. You could say that the personality is just the tip of the iceberg. However, as with the iceberg, the greater portion lies beneath and goes much deeper than the surface.

Consider the following analogy. Before a house is built, the land is cleared in anticipation of the construction. The Designer knew in advance that the house would be built. In fact, the Designer knew everything about this house down to the smallest detail. A builder has the blueprints. Like the watch in a previous example, the house will not be the product of random occurrences, but will be built in a specific order. Even the wiring will be done specific to the unique design and layout of the house. You get the picture.

Once the building site is prepared, what is the first step? That would be laying the foundation which will support the structure. It will hold up the entire weight of the house. Even though parts of the building may extend out over the foundation, the integrity of the structure is dependent upon its foundation. Let us assume that the One Who laid the foundation knew what He was doing. Therefore, the foundation was perfectly designed for its intended purpose. That foundation must exist before anything else can be built upon it. In reality, the foundation remains for the life of the property. Remember, this is just an analogy.

As the construction continues, we see the outline of the building appear. As the framing is completed, not only can we see the outside take shape but the inside as well. Doors, windows, and the layout of each of the interior rooms begins to take shape. All of this follows the blueprint as created by the Architect. In our illustration, we would compare the Architect to the Great Designer. All of this takes place within the womb of the mother where we were *fearfully and wonderfully made* (Ps. 139:14). Consider here David's words to God, "For you formed my inward parts; you knitted me together in my mother's womb" (Ps.139:13 ESV).

We were fully designed individuals when we were created at which time our *body*, *soul*, and *spirit* came together to form us as a unique creation. It is because of this viewpoint that Temperament Therapy differs from secular psychology. The former considers all three while the latter considers only the *body* and the *soul*. We will consider the implications of this difference in greater detail.

The atheist's view sees man as part of the animal and environment that has evolved over millennia. The theist's view believes that animals, although creatures of God, do not have a *spirit*. They only have a *soul* and a *body*. That is the distinguishing factor between mankind and animals. For clarification, *the soul* is often referred to as *the mind* while *the body* is often referred to as *the flesh*.

The Bible tells us that man was created in the *image*

of God (*cf.* Gen. 1:26. 27, 5:3, 9:6). Here we are using the word *man* in the generic sense meaning *mankind* or *humankind*. The word *image* means *likeness*. The Bible refers to Adam as the *son of God* because he was made in the likeness of God and God is a Spirit. This is the point of divergence for those who try to understand and explain man. Man has either evolved like all the other animals from some unknown origin or he is a masterpiece created in the likeness of his Creator. The implications of this choice are far-reaching in one's view of man.

The Bible records man's creation in Genesis 2:7:

> 7 And the LORD God formed man of the dust of the ground, and breathed into his nostrils the breath of life; and man became a living soul.

You may recall these words are often recited at grave-side funerals, "Ashes unto ashes; dust unto dust" and attendees, who choose to do so, take a handful of dirt symbolically throwing it on top of the deceased's coffin. Archaic as that may seem, it is derived from the concept that our body was made from dirt and unto dirt our body shall return.

Have you ever seen a newborn baby and heard

someone say that he or she is the "spitting image" of one of its parents? It makes no sense. Who's spitting? It is actually a derivation of an Old English phrase "spirit and image." We were made to be in the *spirit and image of our Father.* Like our Creator Who is indivisibly comprised of three entities: the Father, the Son, and the Spirit, we too are comprised of three divisible parts. Why do I say divisible? We read in Hebrews 4:12:

> 12 For the word of God is quick, and powerful, and sharper than any two-edged sword, piercing even to the dividing asunder of soul and spirit, and of the joints and marrow, and is a discerner of the thoughts and intents of the heart.

Here, the word *quick* means *living.* The Word of God is alive and powerful. It is capable of dividing between the *soul* and the *spirit.* Although the soul and the spirit may seem like they are the same, the Word of God is able to both discern and divide them one from the other. We will examine the *body*, *soul*, and *spirit* individually going forward.

The Bible uses specific words when revealing or explaining difficult concepts. We know what the *body* means. It means the *flesh.* The Bible uses this word to explain the weakness of man concerning sin. We read in the Gospel of Matthew 26:41:

> 41 Watch and pray, that ye enter not into temptation: the spirit indeed is willing, but the flesh is weak.

Again, we read in the Gospel of Mark 14:38:

> 38 Watch ye and pray, lest ye enter into temptation. The spirit truly is ready, but the flesh is weak.

This weakness of the flesh is the result of our fallen state. Adam and Eve made a choice. They wanted to be like God by having the knowledge of Good and Evil. Having this knowledge, they became prone to choose evil over good. There was only one thing they were told not to do. Here are God's specific instructions to the pair along with His caution of its consequences. We cannot say they were not warned. It is recorded for us in Genesis 2:17:

> 17 But of the tree of the knowledge of good and evil, thou shalt not eat of it: for in the day that thou eatest thereof thou shalt surely die.

To tie this all together, the Apostle Paul writes "For the wages of sin is death . . ." (Rom. 6:23). Here, the word *wages* can be interpreted as meaning *consequence* or *payment for an action*. Today, we are still suffering the consequences from our original parents' choice.

We are not trying to make this book into a theological study. However, it is impossible to explain the temperament without knowing the Creator and understanding the significance of the *Fall of Man*. This becomes more evident as we look at the five individual temperaments and see how sin affects each of them in different ways. We are who we are because that is how we were created. All that God created was good, but sin corrupted it. To understand who we are, we need all the information that applies to us.

The *body* is a *tabernacle*. The word *tabernacle* is used in the Bible meaning a *dwelling place*. The tabernacle that Israel built in the wilderness was a place where God could *dwell with His people*. Our body is the dwelling place for our spirit and, should we accept God's gracious offer of salvation, therein also will the Holy Spirit dwell in us.

The two remaining components are the soul and the spirit. In Genesis we read, "And the LORD God formed man of the dust of the ground, and breathed into his nostrils the breath of life; and man became a living soul" (v. 2:7). When God breathed the breath of life into Adam, he became a *living being*. Let us return to the building again as our illustration. The building is complete and ready for occupancy, but there is no life yet. When the Builder flips the master switch on the electrical panel, all the lights come on. Figuratively, it brings life to the building.

Our thoughts and intellect are stored in our mind. Animals have minds too. We can see this as they look for food, produce offspring, care for and defend themselves. They also have memories of people, places, and things. You could say that their natural instincts are stored in their minds.

The final part is the *spirit*. This is unique to humans. The Greek word for *spirit* is *pneuma*. It can mean spirit, wind, and breath almost interchangeably. You could say that Adam received his *spirit* when God breathed in him the breath of life. Here is an interesting quote from Jesus in the Gospel of John 6:63:

> 63 It is the spirit that quickeneth; the flesh profiteth nothing: the words that I speak unto you, they are spirit, and they are life.

There is that word again. The word *quicken* means *come to* or *bring to life*. So, Jesus is telling His listeners that it is the Spirit that brings life. There is no value to the flesh. The words of the Spirit are, in fact, life itself. Whether breathed or spoken, it is God and His Word that bring things to life. Take a moment and think about that.

At the moment of your conception, God spoke and instantly you became a living creature. It was not a chemical reaction of an amalgamation of fluids or the random outcome from an unknown source. It was done intentionally in the same manner as it was done in the first divine decree of creation. Genesis 1:3–4:

> 3 And God said, Let there be light: and there was light. 4 And God saw the light, that it was good: and God divided the light from the darkness.

Therefore, we believe we were created in His image. We possess a *spirit* and a *soul* which are housed inside this frail human *body*. However, because of sin, our body or *flesh* has a limited life span. It will deteriorate and, eventually, fail. Our spirit and soul which were created in His image will endure forever because we share in His likeness. He wired us before birth with a unique temperament. Discovering who you are will be an exciting journey! Let us start that journey by explaining what exactly is a *temperament*.

4

What Is The Temperament?

How Am I Wired? was created to provide you with an introduction to the concept of our unique wiring inherent in each of us. As such, we must limit the scope of our presentation to the basics. The appendix provides contact information for the National Christian Counselors Association. On their website, you will find a link to a directory of licensed Temperament Therapist.

We will begin with a quick review of what we have learned so far. As previously stated, there are five temperaments and, within each of these, there are three areas of application. The five temperaments, listed below, will be presented alphabetically so as not to imply importance or value to any one of them in particular:

- Choleric
- Melancholic
- Phlegmatic
- Sanguine
- Supine

The temperaments are presented in the form of a grid. To understand the concepts, meanings are placed on the extremes of each side of the grid. Like any graph, individual temperaments can be plotted within the grid. This gives a visual understanding of where someone is located in relationship to the whole. An important point to remember is that one temperament is neither better nor worse than another. That would be like saying that a four-wheel drive pick-up is better than a two-door sports car. Both vehicles have their advantages and disadvantages. However, one might serve a purpose better than the other for specific situations. If you are in the process of moving a piano, the pick-up would clearly be a better choice than the convertible.

Each side of the grid represents a leading dynamic of someone's temperament. There are many titles we could use to caption them. However, we will use a common language approach. These will be used as broad generalizations. Because the following is an important point, you will hear it repeated going forward. The word is *tendencies*. Nothing is written in stone. No one will be pigeon-holed into a box. We truly are individuals with freewill.

Here is a surprising fact. Although we inherit certain attributes such as our physical appearance from our parents, our temperament is unique and given to us directly from God. Parents often look at their child and say that the child looks like them. However, they are perplexed when the child acts or thinks in ways foreign to the parent. Sometimes, they have no idea who this child really is. The answer is that their child came from God and, as such, their child is uniquely wired and different from his or her parents. Here is another benefit to temperament therapy. Not only can it help us to understand ourselves better, it also helps us to understand the unique temperaments of others. That includes our own children.

Let's take a look at the diagram below. The four corners and the center portion represent the five temperaments we will discuss. We can move from a passive and more introverted position to a more assertive and more extroverted position. As we study the grid, you will note that those on the top are focused on people while those at the bottom are focused on tasks. In much the same way, those on the right are more outgoing and those on the left are more reserved. Again, there is neither quality nor value assigned to any area of the grid. We should see everything in this grid as degrees of intensity the further we move toward the edges. The closer one gets to the center, the more balanced one becomes. By remembering this grid going forward, you will find it easier to understand its application.

The Temperament Grid

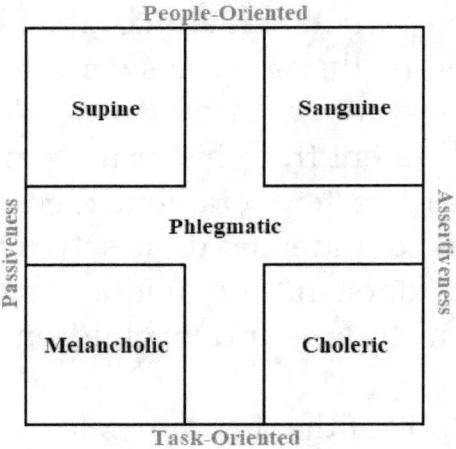

The above is a basic representation of the five temperaments as conceived by the Drs. Richard and Phyllis Arno. However, for clinical purposes, the grid is divided into 100 cells similar to a graph which serve as locators for measurements obtained from the Arno Profile System (APS). Counselors trained and certified in the testing process plot the results on this more precise grid. Temperament Therapists use it as a tool to explain and teach an individual's temperament.

The result is a visual representation of the client's temperament measured in three distinct areas: *Inclusion*, *Control*, and *Affection*. We will look at each of these components to gain a better understanding of what each of them comprises. As humans, we are all fearfully and wonderfully made. We are complex, but we can receive reassurance from the words in Psalm 100:3:

> 3 Know ye that the LORD he is God: it is he that hath made us, and not we ourselves . . .

Within these three areas of *Inclusion*, *Control*, and *Affection*, two measurements are taken. The first is called *expressed*. This measures the level the individual wishes to give or exercise in a particular area. Think of this as outgoing action towards someone else. The second is called *wanted*. This measures the level the individual wishes to receive in that same area. You can think of that as the need, want, or desire to receive. Don't worry. We will explain how this is applied below.

Inclusion

What is *Inclusion?* The best way to explain it is in the words of the Arnos. They define *Inclusion* as the "Temperament area that indicates a need to establish and maintain satisfactory relationships with people regarding surface relationships, association and socialization. This also includes intellectual energies."[1]

You could say this is the manner in which we interact with the world around us. Each of us has a different outlook, view, or perception as we choose either to participate or avoid interaction. How we reach those thoughts is determined by how we choose, by our temperament, to interact with society in general. Many of our social skills, our consciousness, and our desire to deal with the world at large are determined by our position on the temperament grid relative to *Inclusion.* This can range from being an extrovert to an introvert and from the relative importance we place on people or tasks.

Control

Control refers to the extent of control we desire to have over the environment in which we exist. This

---

[1] Richard Gene Arno and Phyllis Jean Arno (Sarasota, Fla.: Peppertree Press, 2018) 2nd ed., 231.

could include the orderliness of our living space or the the way we manage our life. To explain *Control*, we turn to the definition written by the Arnos. In their words *Control* is defined as the ". . . area that indicates a need to establish and maintain satisfactory relationships with people in respect to power and control and decision making abilities, willingness to take on responsibilities and the need for independence."[2]

Control, like the other components of the temperament, can be measured. It has a range from low to high desire to control (1) ourself and (2) others. We can all think of different people with control issues. He or she could be seen as a dominant or assertive person sometimes forcefully achieving their purpose. That is just one example of people whose temperament is in the lower right corner of the grid marked as task-oriented and assertive. However, each of us places somewhere on the grid for *Control*. In the coming chapters, we will start with understanding ourselves before we move on to trying to understand others.

Affection

The final component of the temperament is *Affection*.

---

[2] Ibid., 229.

The Arnos define *Affection* as the "Temperament area that indicates [the] need for love and affection and [the] need to establish and maintain deep, personal relationships with people. This includes physical demonstration (touching, holding hands, etc.) and emotional openness."[3]

As *Inclusion* measures our level of interest to participate with society in general, the area of *Affection* deals specifically with those much closer to us: friends and family. You might refer to them as your immediate circle where the world encompasses a far greater circle of people. We may not value the opinions of those with whom we do not have a close relationship. However, those within our immediate circle are much more likely to have an impact on us. That influence could affect our actions, our emotions, and our thoughts.

Thus far we have laid out the basic concepts of Temperament Therapy in order to lay the groundwork. Going forward, we can now discuss in greater detail the individual temperaments and how they are placed within the Temperament Grid.

---

[3] Ibid., 228.

5

Temperament Overview

As mentioned previously, there are five temperaments. However, there is an almost un-limited number of combinations with varying degrees of intensity in the three areas of *Inclusion*, *Control*, and *Affection*. We must never be tempted to pigeon-hole anyone. We will continue to repeat one important word as we go through the different temperaments. That word is *tendency*. An individual's temperament is measured and analyzed. Then, it is plotted on the grid for a graphical illustration. Its location on the grid shows their indicated temper-ament. Each of these temperaments has its own *strengths* and *weaknesses*.

As we continue with each temperament, it will be easier for you to find it on The Temperament Grid shown in the previous chapter. It will help you to see the changes between the side-to-side and the up-and-down on the grid. From left to the right, it moves from being passive to being assertive. From bottom to top, it changes from being task-oriented to people-oriented. Before we jump to explaining the differences between the temperaments, we thought it might be helpful to give you a real life example of how the analysis of temperaments can be beneficial. First, it helps individuals understand who they are. Second, it helps them to understand that others think and act differently as well as the reason why. The following example shows how an overall poor situation in a working environment can be made better using Temperament Therapy.

Bill is the president of a family-run business. He is the fourth generation to own the company so the roots go deep. Bill's wife Susan was made the bookkeeper because he trusted her. He expected her to sit at her desk near the receiving dock and crunch numbers, pay bills, and do all the tasks someone in accounting would do. However, she was spending a lot of her time in the sales department encouraging the sales people and talking with customers. The accounting work was not getting done. When Bill talked with his wife she became angry and depressed. She had never told him that she hated her job.

Now, let us look at the grid. Think about what type of person an accounting job required. It needed a detailed person, someone who was patient, good with numbers, and accurate. That would be a task-oriented person and someone more passive than outgoing. That would be a Melancholic.

Susan is the head of the PTA at her children's elementary school. At church, she is the first one to volunteer to head a committee or fund drive. She is on the phone with her girlfriends at night and has lunch with one or two of them each week. She loves people and is quick to get involved with forming or leading a group. She tested on the APS as a Sanguine. Susan loves people and thrives whether making new relationships or strengthening existing ones.

Bill had a problem. As the president, he is trying to put a square peg into a round hole. He needs a Melancholic to handle his accounting, but his wife is a Sanguine. There was nothing wrong with her. It was just a mismatch. You can see how important understanding a temperament is. It can affect your quality of life both physically and emotionally if you are out of sync with your temperament.

The story continues. Bill was going to let one of his sales staff go because he was taking too much time to make each sales. Marty's sales figures were too low for what he was being paid. Marty was methodical, extremely accurate, and documented all his conversations with clients in great detail. He would arrive early and go home late, but his sales numbers were still too low. To make matters worse, Marty dreaded coming to work each day. We did a temperament assessment on Marty and the report revealed that his temperament was a Compulsive Melancholic. That is someone who was extremely task-oriented, an introvert, and certainly not outgoing. He is the exact opposite of Susan and the perfect temperament for an accountant. Bill agreed to cross-train his wife and Marty. That was three years ago. Susan and Marty are both very happy with their new positions. Susan has become their top sales person. Marty is an excellent bookkeeper and saved Bill a lot of money with his analytical skills. We will just say that Bill is very pleased with the results.

We can see how the proper application of an individual's temperament to a specific situation is important for two reasons. First, by correctly matching the temperament with the task, the quality and/or quantity of the work increases. Second, the needs of the individual are also fulfilled. This would be a win-win situation. Later on, we will go into greater detail of the individual needs of each temperament.

God created each of us. Therefore, He understands our temperaments: our natural strengths and weaknesses. He also knows how we will react in any given situation. He chooses people, with all their flaws and imperfections, to carry out His purpose. We were created by and wired by God. He knows our schematics as only the Designer can. He knows each of us intimately and, yet, He still loves us. Each individual is unique, created and wired by God, and is loved by God. When we understand someone's temperament, we can see them as God sees them. Not only will it help us to understand ourselves, it will also change the way we see others!

We want you to understand the material presented in this book and continue to learn more. It becomes a study in humanity. You can contact the National Christian Counselors Association for more information. Their website is https://www.ncca.org. They provide access to resources and courses in temperament training.

Think about the people recorded in the Bible. We sometimes forget they were created like us. For a moment, assume that Moses was a Melancholic. He was passive, quiet, and an introvert. As a Melancholic, Moses would have been extremely detailed in his tasks. That would be necessary for someone to write down word-for-word exactly what God dictated to him. It required great precision and great patience. To assist him, God appointed his brother Aaron to be his spokesperson. Later, in the heat of confrontation with Pharoah, Moses would speak with confidence. Everyone has limitations. God knows this and provides.

The Apostle Peter represents the Sanguine. He was fearless and outspoken with people. Think of the confidence in his speech at Pentecost. Speaking before the crowds, he was certainly bold. Then, there is the story about two sisters, Mary and Martha. Martha was working diligently to prepare the meal as her sister Mary sat at Jesus' feet listening to Him. Martha was task-oriented while Mary was passive. She cared about people especially Jesus. Martha was hard at work in the kitchen. Her boldness to complain to Jesus indicates she may have been a Choleric. Mary was most likely a Supine. These people we remember favorably, but not all temperaments belong to good people.

Consider Pharaoh. He was task-oriented and had no intention of losing power or control of his vast empire. This especially applied to his massive labor pool of Hebrew slaves. Pharoah considered himself to be god and no one was going to take that away from him. He was not a people-oriented person. He was a very dynamic example of a Choleric. But, God can use every situation and temperament to achieve His will. Pharaoh's opposition to God allowed Him the perfect situation to display His divine power to the known world. God was to be respected.

To counter any negativity being associated with the Choleric temperament, the Apostle Paul was no doubt a Choleric as well. He was highly educated and focused his religious piety on persecuting the Kingdom Church. Cholerics find changing their opinions or beliefs extremely difficult. Sometimes, that is a good thing. God had to use thunder, lightning, and blinding Paul to get his attention. The gospel message Paul received from Christ was contrary to what was previously known. God needed someone with Paul's focus, determination, and drive to carry His message. (*cf.* Gal. 1:11-18.) Each person in the Bible fell short of God's perfection. Each had a temperament. Although we cannot be one-hundred percent sure, we can guess which temperament they had. This brings us to an important point.

Once we have a general understanding of the temperaments including their tendencies, strengths, and weaknesses, we are cautioned not to "guess." People tend to look at someone's outward appearance and actions. The temperament like an iceberg is mostly concealed. Therefore it is dangerous to "guess" because ten out of ten times we will most likely be wrong. Many new counselors have been tempted to try this. Although specifically instructed in their training, they privately and without voicing their thoughts to anyone, guess that a person must be a "this" or a "that." Temperaments are hidden deep under the character and personality of the individual. We can only see the top layer. We have already described the *personality* as our *public persona*. It is referred to as "the mask" which we wear in public. Again, think of an iceberg. What we see on the top–what is visible to our observation–is nowhere near what lies beneath the surface. So heed our warning and avoid the temptation to misjudge someone's temperament. Only an APS diagnostic report can reveal what truly lies beneath the visible surface.

Going forward, the temperaments will be presented in alphabetical order. This way, there is no greater importance or emphasis placed on any one of them. There will be two chapters for each of the five core temperaments. A general overview of the temperament will be presented first. Then the following chapter will provide a real life example. We will see how Temperament Therapy can be applied to various situations.

With this in mind, let us get started by discovering more about these wonderful God-given temperaments.

Introducing The Choleric

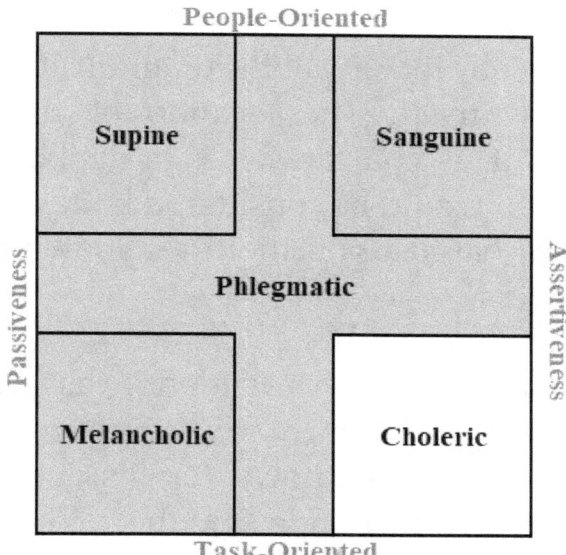

The importance of the following statement cannot be overstressed. Everything we attribute to this temperament, as well as the four that follow, will introduce you to a list of tendencies, predispositions, or inclinations. The summaries will provide an explanation or analysis of the *tendencies* of a particular temperament although they will vary in degree of their intensity. There is that word again: *tendency*. Please remember this as we go forward.

Introduction

In this chapter, we will consider how the Choleric is wired as well as some of their strengths and weaknesses.

You can start by looking at the diagram above to help acclimate yourself. The location of the Choleric temperament, as you can see, is in the bottom right. That position would be considered both *assertive* and *task-oriented* based upon the titles shown along the grid's borders.

One historical person we can identify as a Choleric is General George Patton, a US Army general from World War II. He is known for his get-it-done-at-any-cost temperament. He saw the soldiers as tools to accomplish his goal. When he visited an army hospital he berated a soldier suffering from severe shell shock calling him a coward. His words made headlines on most of the newspapers back in the

States and it became a public relations problem. His commanding officer forced him to apologize publically. Patton had focused on the objective and forgotten about the people. This tends to happen with Cholerics.

If there is something that you absolutely must get done and there is a deadline, call upon a Choleric. They will get it done. There is a saying about asking a Choleric. "There might be dead bodies, but the task will be done on schedule and under budget." In general, Cholerics are known as drivers.

General Tendencies of The Choleric

We will generally find that a Choleric is not a "people person" although they can be quite personable when the task requires it. They usually have an agenda and are not free with sharing it. They hold themselves to a high standard of effectiveness and efficiency. It can be difficult to have a relationship with them. They are generally closed and highly focused. Should they take on an assignment or task, it will be for a specific reason and they very rarely give up. They are driven by a need for accomplishment and that need is never-ending. They will generally multi-task and possibly look down on those who are not equally as busy.

It is not that they do not like people, but in their view, people are either a distraction or an obstacle around which they must circumnavigate. Because of their drive, they seek reward through acknowledgment for their actions. They like recognition and praise. Lack of recognition will cause irritation and even anger. Anger does seem to be a predominant factor in the nature of their responses.

They think intuitively. Assessing a situation and identifying possible actions appears easy for them. This is due to their ability to think on their feet. Unlike the Melancholic who is also a thinker, the Choleric is a quick decision-maker. They think clearly and decisively. In a country church there was no one willing to take on the Easter breakfast following the sunrise service. It was way too early. One woman stepped to the plate and said she would do it. Seventy or so people walked into the church's fellowship hall on a cold rainy day. They all wanted Easter breakfast at the same time. They were cold, wet, and hungry. Someone stood in the middle of the church's kitchen and asked this woman how could they help. In a very concise and honest manner, she said, "Well, you can start by getting out of my way." She is a great lady and much loved because she calls it the way she sees it. When a Choleric is working, the best thing you can do is get out of their way.

A Choleric is personable and much of the time charismatic in their demeanor. Most people like them because of their dynamics and charm. However, to the Choleric, people are sometimes seen as a tool. The purpose of socializing and associating with others is to accomplish an ulterior motive. The people with whom they choose to surround themselves are usually weaker and easily managed. After a while or when their intended use has ended, these relationships seem to fizzle out. The Choleric may lose respect for the weaker associates even to the point of becoming abusive or demeaning. When confronted with another Choleric, sparks will fly and the situation could get ugly. Once the hierarchy is established and each knows their place, normality will once again return.

A Choleric establishes their own standards. As long as the employee is giving the boss what is expected, within the planned timeframe, and at the expected level of production, things will go smoothly. Rocking the boat or falling short, will result in a swift reprimand with promises of consequences should the problem not be resolved. As far as personal relationships, the Choleric may view emotions and feelings as superfluous and sentimental. They are much like the Scrooge in Dickens' *A Christmas Carol*. However, that character had a change of heart which proves that many of the above tendencies can be altered or controlled. It is our freewill that allows us to choose whether to cling to or change our current outlook.

Among all of the temperaments, the Choleric has the intellect, power, and capacity to be the most destructive. That was not the intent of the Creator Who wired them. The intent was for good and not evil. Each of us has the freewill to make our own choices accordingly. From a theological perspective, following the fall of man when sin entered the world, our natural proclivity or tendency will be to choose evil. It will only be through faith and by seeking guidance from the Creator, that we can alter our desire and choose good.

Strengths and Weaknesses of The Choleric

The Choleric appears to be happy, well-adjusted, confident, focused, driven, and out-going. They can assess a situation, make a thorough analysis, and come up with the best immediate solution faster than any other temperament. Will it be the right choice of action? Perhaps, but based on the immediacy of the situation or the acute nature of the crisis, they will adapt after they set about to accomplish the solution.

Concerning their potential weaknesses, it seems they

are always close to the boiling point, and if not, can boil pretty quickly. They tend to see people as temporary tools and use them to accomplish their task. They enjoy being in control because of their fear of the unexpected and being a failure to plan appropriately. We were once told by a Choleric, "I don't control. I manage!" We showed her the definition of the verb "to manage." It means "to have charge or administer, to conduct, to exert control over, to regulate or limit toward a desired end, to direct or otherwise supervise." She was silent as she thought about it.

Cholerics will take on tough projects, are good leaders, are quick and decisive, implement changes almost immediately, and have the capacity of dynamite to get things done. A Choleric who is a telephone lineman said he had the perfect job. He gets his work done and, as far as people go, they stay out of his way. Perhaps a perfect tee-shirt for a true Choleric would read, "CAUTION! DOES NOT PLAY WELL WITH OTHERS." Also, if you listen to a Choleric speak or read what they have written informally, you can count the number of times they use the personal pronouns: I, me, my, and mine. For them, they are self-centric in their view of the world.

Cholerics expect you to be honest and direct with them. How can they make the correct decisions if they do not have the most up-to-date and correct information. Therefore, they generally hate surprises since they are unable to plan for contingencies. We should always be straight with them–provide full disclosure. Tell them what you think directly, be honest, but allow at least a six foot space. This is just a bit of humor which is not lost on someone who knows a true Choleric.

Unfortunately, the Choleric's life is sometimes lonely. A common phrase for them would be, "I will be happy when _____." Their perception of life is that it is all about tasks and their self worth is derived from their accomplishments. Many times their recreation is designed with a purpose of achieving some end. They also see the imperfections in life as measured against perfection as they see it. As a result, they can have issues with depression and becoming burnt out. Even when burnt out, they will faithfully continue since the work never ends.

The value of the Choleric cannot be overstated. They are usually very intelligent, tend to have excellent communication skills, have the ability to react quickly and decisively in most situations, and remain committed to completing their objectives. Temperament Therapists will value the Choleric. They can work with them to identify issues and provide suggestions on how they can best deal with their own temperament's predispositions. They need to understand that maintaining their physical and mental health is critical. In the next chapter, we will look at how to understand the Choleric temperament and how they can successfully adapt by knowing how they are wired.

In the following chapters we will introduce each of the five major temperaments. Then, we follow it with another chapter providing a counseling example of that temperament. These are actual people who worked with one of the authors in temperament counseling. Of course their personal information has been changed to protect their identities. Each example will be presented by one of the authors who had the privilege of getting to know and counsel the client.

An assessment will be completed using the Arno Profile System (APS). This report will focus on three areas of their temperament. We will briefly review them again to refresh your memory. The three areas are: *Inclusion*, *Control*, and *Affection*. *Inclusion* is the individual's desire or need for social interaction as well as their intellectual energy. *Control* is their disposition to make decisions and their willingness to take responsibility for themselves as well as responsibility for others. *Affection* is their desire to give and receive affection, love, and acceptance. This area relates to the need for meaningful personal relationships.

Life certainly provides its challenges. We are faith-based counselors and, as Temperament Therapists, we always turn to the most knowledgeable source of anything created–the Manufacturer. You might ask, "Who is that?" It is God–the Creator. Temperament Therapists are only a facilitator because, as we believe, the actual healing or solution comes from the Creator Himself.

7

An Example Of The Choleric

As we mentioned before, when it comes to examining the temperaments of actual people, there are thousands of possibilities. This is what makes each person a unique creation. Therefore, it is almost impossible to find someone with a pure unblended temperament. In the examples, we will see that each person is a composite of temperament types expressed in the three areas of *Inclusion*, *Control*, and *Affection*. Rather than a clinical study, we will present our examples to you in a narrative format. Everyone likes a story, right?

I would like to introduce you to our first client. His name is Edmond, he is 56 years old, and is married. He was born in a city formerly a mill town in New England where he owns a successful business with approximately seventy employees. He has four children and has been married to his wife Alicia for thirty-two years. All of their children are now adults and live more than several hours from their parents. This may stem from the fact that they all attended college at a distance from home. At first the children would regularly return with their spouses for all the major holidays and birthdays, but now only one child visits them with their family each summer. The others exchange phone calls with their mother regularly and speak to the father rarely.

Edmond continues to work six days a week at the business. Alicia has asked multiple times to visit the children especially during the summer months, but Edmond refuses. His response was, "A wife belongs with her husband." She has offered to cook sufficiently in advance and arrange for someone to keep the house clean. Again, he refused. He arranged a meeting in my office and explained the situation. He expressed his expectation that, as a Christian counselor, I should explain to Alicia that her place is with her husband. I think that briefly summarizes the situation and reason for counseling in a nutshell.

In advance of this first meeting, Edmond had reluctantly completed the APS assessment. I say reluctantly because he made it clear from the beginning that there was nothing wrong with him. In our meeting, I listened and sat there for a moment. Then I asked him a question, "Did you provide for the needs of your children while they were growing up?" There was a bit of indignance in his voice when he replied that he most assuredly did. I began with a list and waited for his answer of yes: you housed them, clothed them, provided them with a safe and comfortable house, fed them; met their educational needs? The list was much longer than this and it took some time, but he answered yes to each. I acknowledged his response with some remark of admiration. My pace was slow, but I had a specific point I was about to make.

I finally told him, "Edmond, you are an excellent provider and protector. You have successfully raised four children all fruitful with families of their own." I asked him about who handled the children's emotional needs growing up. To which, he informed me that it was Alicia's job. For a Choleric, everything in life is seen as a task. I was confident that together they were an excellent team. God does tend to pair opposites. Now came my most important question, "So who takes care of Alicia's emotional needs?" There was silence. Sometimes the hardest part for me as a counselor is knowing when to shut up and let God speak to his heart. I can still remember those five minutes being the longest time I had waited for an answer. He did eventually answer that he was the one who needed to take care of her needs.

I met with Edmond nine times after that during which time I learned a lot about him. During our sessions, I gave him the affirmation and acknowledgment for his accomplishments which he needed to hear. He was the family's provider and protector. He worked six days a week and took the family to church on Sunday mornings. Sunday afternoon was his time to watch sports and have a beer. The bills were paid. They lived in a beautiful four-bedroom home with a built-in swimming pool. He planned to sell his business someday as none of his children were interested in running the family business. It would be sold for enough money to provide for their retirement with a sizeable inheritance for each of their children. I totally understood his drive, his work ethic, and his dedication to accomplishing the tasks which he believed God had given him. For him, it was a sense of duty.

I presented the counseling sessions to Edmond as a consultant hired to help him make a decision. One does not tell a Choleric what to do! However, you may suggest. We were, figuratively, sitting on the same side of the table. This would be a project we would be working on together. There was another reason Edmond did not want Alicia to leave. He was a Supine in *Affection*. That is the exact opposite of the Choleric. He needed her emotionally. He was connected to her and loved her dearly. In fact, he would not have been able to accomplish everything he had without her constant affection and encouragement.

The challenge for a Temperament Therapist is not to judge the client but rather to understand who God made them to be. As our sessions came closer towards a solution, he was able to see that without the children Alicia's tasks were complete. She had been home alone six days a week for the last five years and she was missing the chance to see her grandchildren grow up. He still wanted to be her provider and protector. He definitely loved her. Knowing that, we set about to establish another task for Edmond. Yes, another task, but one he could easily handle. I was talking to him in a way he could understand. We made a plan!

Edmond agreed he would take his wife to see each of their children for one to two weeks. They would stay at nearby hotels or bed & breakfasts. He would have his wife every night to himself. He would provide her with transportation to and from the hotel. He would be there for her and provide for her needs.

Could Edmond change into somebody else? He had a powerful temperament and changing him would have been next to impossible. However, he was willing to adapt the situation to one that would be tolerable, perhaps even enjoyable, for him. The last session before their first trip, I met with both him and his wife. He had his loving affectionate wife back who was now extremely happy.

I did make a few suggestions to them both so that they were both on the same page. Edmond needed to understand that when they visited their children's home, this is someone else's ship and someone else is the captain. Also, you are not to arrive as the admiral. I asked him if he understood knowing full well that his listening wife might have to remind him again later. Next, put it on your task list to tell your children that you have always loved them, but you showed your love by providing for and protecting them. Tell them that you now understand you are a task-oriented person.

Since it is important for you to be "doing" something, ask if there are any projects that need to be done while you are there visiting. Tell them that is your way of showing them that you love them. There may be a chance that some of your grandchildren might be task-oriented and want to help. Let them. It is their way of showing you that they love you. I printed out these suggestions, handed them to him and told him to let me know how things went when he got back.

The Choleric is the most difficult to counsel. It is like changing cured cement. They speak "task" and understand life in that framework. They also need to be validated. I was blessed to have known Edmond from church and, therefore, I had established a level of trust with him. However, a Choleric does not take advice from just anyone. They want credentials. They will consider professional advice but only from experienced advisors. I approached Edmond as a trusted advisor. He knew he needed something, but was not sure how to get it. We turned meeting Alicia's need into a task he would willingly complete. We looked at what needed to be accomplished. Those were the tasks. Then, we talked about how this could be achieved and keep Edmond happy as well.

All of this occurred a few years ago. As of the writing of this book, I had received a letter from Alicia saying that Edmond had decided to sell the business and move them closer to two of their children. They plan on visiting each of them on a regular basis and the children are looking forward to their visits as projects always get done when Dad is there.

It is important to understand that a Choleric sees their work personae as who they are. They are driven to accomplish as this is how they feel people will judge them. They also have a natural inclination to solve problems which they see as personal challenges. As such, their fear is that if they fail, fall short, or drop their mask, people will see them for who they really are. They may not even be sure who that really is.

Their fear of failure is very real and, therefore, they tend to have a fragile self-esteem. Edmond needed to understand who God created him to be. His family loves him. They are the safest people with whom he can be himself and not his work personae, but that will take time. He needs to be open and tell his family about who God created him to be. He cannot change who he is, but he can adapt. Striving to be a perfectionist will only lead to failure and disappointment. As a human, he is not perfect. Only God is perfect and Edmond needed to accept that.

As Temperament Therapists, we do not try to change people into someone else. Edmond listened to Bible verses and we always prayed together. We asked God to help Edmond solve his problem with his wife and family. I believe that God did and so does he. I always remind my clients to thank God and share with others what God has done for them.

Submitted by,
David A. Greene, Ph.D.

8

Introducing The Melancholic

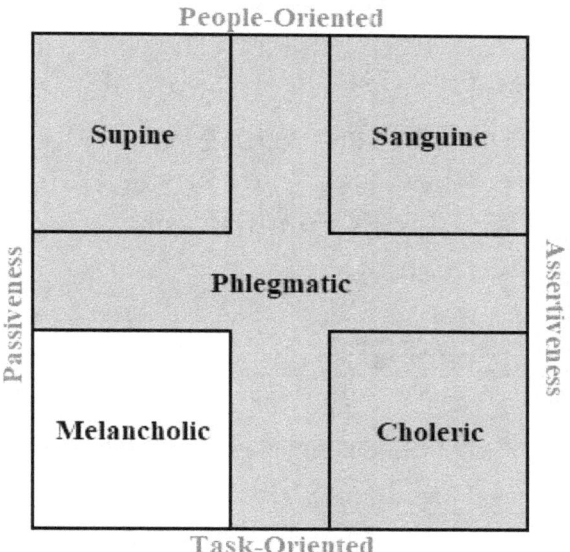

In this chapter, we will examine the Melancholic. Their *tendencies* are also based upon their unique wiring.

Introduction

As with each temperament, the strengths and weaknesses of the Melancholic are different. However, they share some commonality with the Choleric. To explain, look at the diagram above. Notice that the Melancholic and Choleric are both located in the lower quadrants of the diagram. This makes them both task-oriented. However, we will see their approaches to tasks are different. The Melancholic is more passive while the Choleric is more assertive. This sharing of tendencies or traits applies when looking at any two adjacent temperament styles. While the Melancholic and Sanguine are complete opposites as is the case with Choleric and Supine. However, as they say, "opposites attract." This brings a diversity of strengths and weaknesses to a team along with challenges.

General Tendencies of The Melancholic

The Melancholic is considered to be both *passive* and *task-oriented*. Their temperament uses a slower pace and they are more methodical in their approach than the Choleric. Still they are both task-oriented. The Melancholic will be detailed, accurate, and a thinker. For them, arriving at the correct solution or answer is far more important than the speed of the process or analysis. The Choleric might see the Melancholic as being too slow or as a procrastinator. This may become the case as they are noted for their desire to obtain and study an unending source of additional information. They have the tendency to review as much information as possible before coming to a conclusion or making a decision. What appears as procrastination is not laziness but rather a desire to be thorough. They work hard to make the "right" decision. A Melancholic tends to be highly intellectual and a conceptual thinker. A Choleric and a Melancholic might work well together if they both agree the Choleric is the boss.

The Melancholic is often beleaguered by self-doubt and low self-esteem. They have a fear of being rejected by people and are typically very sensitive to criticism. Because they are perfectionists, they establish a very high standard for themselves. This almost always sets them up for failure or disappointment, but yet they persevere. Of all the temperaments, they are the ones who tend to be the most critical of themselves. This leads them to take the safest position by being an introvert. By doing this, others typically see them as haughty and someone who thinks they are superior to others. However, that is far from being the case.

When working with others, they tend to be very direct in stating facts. They do this without consideration of other's emotions. Growing up, you may remember Mr. Spock, first officer of the Enterprise. He would make an excellent example of a Melancholic. He was extremely accurate and highly logical in everything that he did. However, he lacked the emotions with which to interact with other humans. Since his mother was human, as the series developed, he tried and succeeded in accessing those emotions.

The Melancholic operates internally–in their own world. They are usually happy to be left alone to think, research, and learn. They are private people. When interacting with others, they are happy to provide information and answer questions. In fact, they often live for that purpose whereby they can offer value by being of value to others. However, they are not offended when others do not take their advice. To them, they provided the information and they do not care whether that information is used. They served their function. Unlike the Choleric, they seldom tell others what they should do.

Both the Choleric and Melancholics prefer to be offered options rather than being told what to do. However, Melancholics can tend to be stubborn and very independent, therefore unlikely to either act or change without being allowed to think about it first. When dealing with problems or crises, they may withdraw to contemplate the situation. They may want to be left alone to think.

Another unique tendency of the Melancholic is their ability to recall memories in great detail. For them, it is as if it were recorded with both audio and video. When they think about past experiences or situations, they will experience the emotions as they recall the events. Their emotions recorded with the event are experienced again as if it was currently happening. If we add to this the self punishment for making mistakes in life, the result is they can be prone to depression. These issues can cause a deterioration in their health as their thoughts spiral downward. As such, they would be more likely to commit suicide than the other temperaments. However, by focusing on their positive accomplishments and how much they are loved by others, they can raise their outlook. This positive reflection changes their attitude and self-worth. Temperament Therapy is usually very effective for the Melancholic because they are willing to listen and learn.

Some of the most gifted people are Melancholics because they are idealists. They are grouped as intellectual and creative. They grasp concepts, ideas, and, as such, they can see completely outside the box. Many composers, artists, sculptors, scientists, and architects are Melancholics. They persist and work at a steady, even pace. Their energies may appear limited, but that is because of the tremendous amount of work their minds are doing. Thomas Edison liked to work long nights in his laboratory when he was alone to think. He often was refreshed by cat-naps or, as we might say, power-naps. His mind never stopped working which can be mentally exhausting.

Concerning socialization, the Melancholic could withdraw either physically, mentally or both. They are usually not expressive when it comes to their emotions or feelings. They have been described as a "home body." They are most comfortable within their own environment which is usually structured and organized. For them, it is a safe place, a refuge from the chaos of the world. Their introvert nature is more applicable to the outside world-at-large. So when it comes to affection, they are generally well-connected to both their family and close friends.

Strengths and Weaknesses of The Melancholic

The value of a Melancholic is their intellectual and creative abilities. They can think in the abstract and envision pitfalls and problems before they happen. They are willing to participate on a team provided they can operate independently, at their own pace, and not feel pressured. Their input will be invaluable. Melancholics have high expectations for themselves especially in areas of tenacity, veracity, and fidelity. Their pursuit of truth and logic are of the utmost importance.

If you are looking for detailed and thorough analysis, the Melancholic is your person. When a question arises, they will consult multiple sources with differing views to come to a conclusion. Many times people will think that the Melancholic is doing nothing. They are just sitting there. However, their mind is busy thinking about a decision or conclusion from multiple angles.

Although the Melancholic is not likely to express their emotions to many, this does not mean that they do not experience emotions. In fact, their feelings run deep. They just lack the knowledge or confidence on how to express their feelings properly. They also fear rejection or ridicule. In spite of this, they make long-term friends who remain both faithful and loyal, perhaps even to their own detriment. They are the friend who is willing to make personal sacrifices on behalf of others. Their choice of friends is highly selective. At first they may be skeptical, believing that someone wants something from them. However, once a bond is created, they make a long-term commitment to maintain that relationship.

Finally, they use a tremendous amount of energy thinking. Usually after stressful situations such as making a public presentation or completing a book, they will need time to recharge their batteries. Spouses can help by giving them time to rest, but also planning social and physical events in advance to include "recharging" time. This will allow for the Melancholic to budget their energy allocation in advance and know that there is a planned time of refreshment coming. This is one of many tools or techniques suggested by a Temperament Therapist. These will help the Melancholic live successfully and happily without changing who they are. The Melancholic is a valuable asset to have as they function within their unique temperament as God created them.

9

An Example Of The Melancholic

The Melancholic is usually an introvert, very smart, or creative person. They are private people. In the following case, the client's APS report revealed that he was a Melancholic, in varying degrees, with all three areas of his temperament: *Inclusion, Control,* and *Affection.* His assessment also revealed that he is a Melancholic Compulsive in *Inclusion.* This is an individual's desire for social interaction and their level of intellectual energy. The word *compulsive* in any temperament description just intensifies the characteristics of the components of this temperament. A Melancholic Compulsive is passive and pushed towards the extreme corner.

Richard is a single business owner in his mid-thirties and has no children. As a business owner, he is always trying to expand his business and, as a result, he was dealing with fear. I began by teaching him about who God created him to be. In the *Inclusion* area, we reviewed his APS report. As we discussed the nature of his temperament, he admitted that he is very task-oriented and self-motivated. A Melancholic is a perfectionist. During our meeting he said he fears rejection. This is typical for Melancholics when they see themselves as having fallen short of other's expectations or demands. They also fear rejection in the area of relationships.

Richard lives alone. This is another characteristic of the Melancholic: the desire to maintain privacy and solitude. In spite of owning and running a business, he is personally very private. He prefers to spend time alone which allows him to think and process. Richard also distrusts people. When he understood that what he was experiencing was natural for the Melancholic, it helped him immensely. He learned that God made him that way for a reason. Having these characteristics was okay. He had weaknesses, but he also had strengths.

Opening up to people had always been a challenge for him, especially as a child. He stated he had no problem with interacting and socializing with people. It was "trusting people" that had always proven to be difficult for him.

We continued by reviewing another component of his temperament in the area of *Control*. Going through the characteristics of *Control*, he was surprised and admitted that these traits were very accurate. He desires little control over the lives and behaviors of others. However, he equally would not tolerate any attempt to be controlled. Some of the traits besides being highly independent and strong-willed helped him to start the business and accomplish other things in his life. He stated he was more comfortable working in well-known areas. When taking on tasks and responsibilities in new areas, he was anxious and uncomfortable. This insecurity was caused by his desire to do everything perfectly.

As an analytical person, he is very quick to pick up and learn, but requires time to become familiar before he gains confidence. The field of his business is familiar to him and he is experienced. Being in control of his circumstances and having the need to appear to be competent is very important to him. Despite the stress of starting a new business, he is tenacious in his pursuit of accomplishing his goals. Melancholics tend to be workaholics, but they have a limited amount of energy. They expend a tremendous amount of mental energy. I suggested time management may be beneficial along with planned rest or recreation. This could be helpful given the stressful situations he may find himself in. He agreed to limit his time when focusing on certain projects. He liked the idea of focusing his time on areas where he is less comfortable. He agreed that with experience he would gain confidence. This helped to reduce the stress in his life.

Next, we focused on the area of *Affection* and the characteristics of his particular temperament. As a Melancholic, he would most likely require a minimal amount of love and affection. On this point, he disagreed. He told me that he does not need a certain amount of love and affection. He has no need for constant reassurance by hugging, touching, or kissing. As a Compulsive Melancholic, this made complete sense. He is currently dating occasionally, but did not have any particular person he wished to discuss. I suggested that explaining his particular temperament to any long-term potential partner would be important for them to understand and accept him.

He told me that his way of expressing his love is by doing special tasks. He would say, "I love you." However, he would not feel the need or desire to say it all the time. I gave him an example of the Sanguine in *Affection*. This person would need constant touching, kissing, and reassurance of being loved by you. He responded with the statement that he would be self-sacrificing for his deep, personal relationships as his way of showing affection. I pointed out that meeting the temperament needs of his life partner could be part of that self-sacrificing.

In our final session, we went over some suggestions to help reduce stress, anxiety and personal interaction. He could set a period of time every day to regenerate, allowing a quiet time to relax and reflect. This should help him reduce stress and clear the mind. I told him it is important for him to have this time set aside each day.

It is important for him to stay positive and take control of his circumstances by taking action once he had fully analyzed the situation. Taking that action will help his business to grow. Also, attempting new things become less stressful. As he gains experience his confidence in the quality of his work will increase. Being alone is good for a Melancholic. It gives them time to think. I explained that learning to trust God with his life and future will help reduce the fear of the unknown. He needs to learn to become secure in God's love. He needs to see himself and others the way God made each of us–as unique creations.

Respectfully submitted,
Eve J. Day, M.A.C.C.

10

Introducing The Phlegmatic

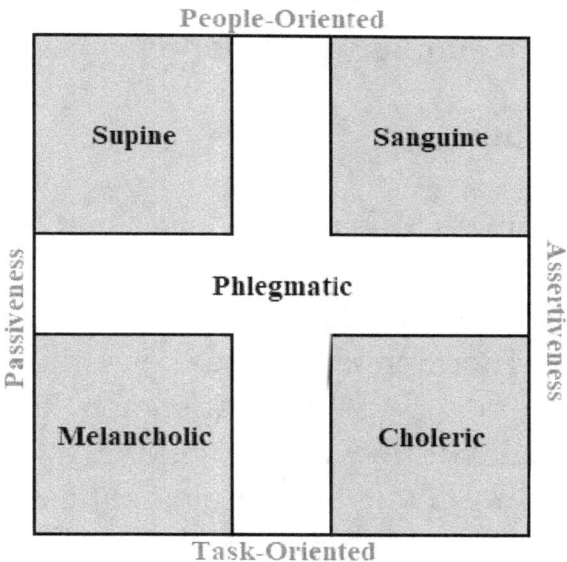

In this chapter, we will introduce the Phlegmatic who is created with their own unique wiring. Their temperament, like the others, will include a list of characteristics which are, as mentioned before, only tendencies.

If you look at the diagram above, you will note that the Phlegmatic holds a very unique position. This illustration may help to understand them better. We can think of it this way: picture a perfectly square table top balanced on the point of a cone. That one point is located in the perfect center of the bottom. In our metaphor, assume that it is perfect because God designed it that way. The role of the Phlegmatic can be seen as a balancer. They are the ones who attempt to maintain equilibrium–balance.

Introduction

The Phlegmatic can best be described as middle-of-the-road or extremely balanced in both their expressed and wanted behavior as seen by the diagram. Their tendency is to be extremely detailed and accurate like the Melancholic which is introverted, but they can be stubborn when it comes to preventing change. The Phlegmatic is the one that tries to hold everything in balance. They like order and also like the status quo. Change, for them, is not seen as a good thing until after it has been success-fully tested; preferably over a long period of time.

Here is another example of the importance of balance in a group dynamic. Looking at the diagram again, picture it being a raft out on a lake that people can swim to for fun. Picture the Phlegmatics congregating in the center. As people with different temperaments move their respective locations on the raft, the balance on the raft changes. The Phlegmatic's role is to find the balance and protect everyone from turning the raft over. With this picture in mind, we can now understand how God uses people of different temperaments to balance the world between the four extremes. In affect, they work together to hold His creation in balance.

We think that the temperament of Phlegmatics is more easily understood when seen in relationship to the whole.

General Tendencies of The Phlegmatic

Overall the Phlegmatic is not too excitable. Maintaining the status quo is important. Changes only are made to the current state of things in a gradual, but tried and tested manner. They may appear to be somewhat uninvolved or detached as they stand back and observe. Rarely are the guardians of balance removed from their post. They generally have a dry or wry sense of humor using it to get their points across without ruffling too many feathers. In fact, many are stand-up comedians. They can observe life and give us their honest commentary in a way that we can all laugh about it.

Their detachment allows them to be good listeners as they remain objective and unmoved. They are not easily swayed, but will only revise their beliefs or thoughts over a period of serious contemplation. They are patient and quite willing to wait to see what others are going to do or say. From that, they will draw their conclusions which are unlikely to change. They are dependable, even-keeled, and loyal. Their work could be described as: neat, well-organized, and accurate. It is done consistently with high standards.

Strengths and Weaknesses of The Phlegmatic

Their balanced nature makes them an excellent choice for highly detailed and tedious tasks. Their work product will tend to be highly accurate. They take pride in this as they feel their work represents them. Therefore, they strive to be perfect by making the correct decision or choice in every area of their life.

Their power of observation and non-involvement in groups presents another aspect of their temperament. They tend to be highly critical when their observations compare people or objects to what they perceive as perfection. That applies to work done by an individual or a group. When asked to participate in a group they will generally procrastinate as they survey the group's proposed activities and members. They will usually enumerate their faults or mistakes, and wait long enough to join in, if they ever do, until the project looks like it will be completed to the Phlegmatic's standards.

Being correct is important to them and it is very hard for them to change their mind. They can be stubborn as they hold onto their convictions. We can see this can be both a strength and a weakness depending on the situation. They have a regimented lifestyle and are very disciplined in their approach to anything they do. Following rules is easy for them. They would not seek to challenge rules or procedures unless it conflicts with their perfectionist's standards.

Much of their energy is consumed by observation and thinking. They will protect their limited amount of energy when planning to become involved in any project. Much thought is done before making a commitment. It is difficult to motivate a Phlegmatic due to this internal thinking process and their concern for their preservation of energy. They may view their world, see the problems, and even know the necessary solutions. However, due to this low energy, they are unlikely to get involved in a leadership position. Since their internal prime directive is to maintain balance or equilibrium, the Phlegmatic hates conflict of any sort. Their ability to detach is a protective mechanism which, if they are not careful, can make them apathetic about life and relationships. However, the Phlegmatic will be a dependable, steady partner and companion running neither too hot nor too cold.

To summarize, Phlegmatics provide stability and balance. Their effect upon a group is to protect against extremes by providing moderation. Like the Melancholic, they have limited energy and do a tremendous amount of thinking. In conflicts or other stressful environments, they will use up their energy quickly and need to recharge. Their energy is best spent on observing, studying, and researching answers to problems or questions.

Their counsel is invaluable to those who seek a balanced and practical approach to any situation. Their low energy and critical nature can cause problems with spouses, coworkers, and friends. The Temperament Therapist can work with the Phlegmatic to refocus their outlook without changing their strengths. Nevertheless, in spite of their weaknesses, they do provide a valuable contribution in service to God and others.

92

11

An Example Of The Phlegmatic

It has been said that out of all the temperaments, the Phlegmatic is both the most stubborn and the most mellow and affable. When thinking of a Phlegmatic, one should think of the word moderate. The Phlegmatic occupies the center of the temperaments for a reason. They are the most balanced, calm, and stable. They take it all in stride. It is very difficult to rattle a Phlegmatic.

In this example of the Phlegmatic temperament, we will meet a 28 year-old electrical engineer. His name is Edward, he is currently engaged, and has no children. His APS report revealed that he is a Phlegmatic in *Inclusion*, Melancholic Phlegmatic in *Control*, and Phlegmatic in *Affection*. When adding a secondary temperament name to a temperament title, such as Melancholic Phlegmatic, it moves the temperament, in this case Phlegmatic, closer to the center of the grid. It makes the temperament less extreme and more balanced.

We began our discussion by explaining the area of *Inclusion*. His job role as an Electrical Engineer requires precision and accuracy. Precision and accuracy take time which is the strength of the Phlegmatic. He told me he felt his career was a perfect match for him. In addition to being able to perform at the high level of precision, his job in engineering does bring with it time pressure. This along with working in unfriendly surroundings he is able to do so with no problem. The Phlegmatic has the ability to function effectively in unfriendly or even hostile surroundings.

Recently, he relocated from Florida to Michigan where he moved to be closer to his fiancée. He was able to adjust well socially and integrate into his new work environment. He said he found the transition fairly easy. He joked and said it was easy to start a new job with fellow engineers because, as he stated, "We are all sarcastic and have a dry sense of humor!" A Phlegmatic will use sarcasm and a dry sense of humor to keep people at a distance. They do this in order to keep others from draining their energy. Engineers require a lot of mental energy and focus. He stated that sometimes his job can be mentally draining. Note that he is a Melancholic Phlegmatic in *Control*. Like the Melancholic, that would include an important need to have control over the quality of his work product.

There is the issue of being stubborn. He said he had spent a lot of time reflecting and thinking over his relocation from Florida to Michigan. He had to weigh out all of his options. He took his time to decide if this was the best decision. Time spent thinking and analyzing options is a trait of a Phlegmatic. Moving to another state was not a small decision. I pointed out that a Phlegmatic will only make a change or a move after fully contemplating detailed analysis and not before. He told me that as an engineer, he feels sometimes that thinking is all he does.

We continued with discussing the area of *Control*. He is self-motivated and likes to make decisions in his own time. He explained that he has always been a self-motivated individual especially when it came to earning his degree and becoming an engineer. Both he and his parents were immigrants. It was difficult with the language barrier, but he did not give up. Everything had to be translated between English and their native language. His parents were both working two jobs in order to support him. His intense studies did not allow time to work and contribute to the household. He said he will always be grateful to his parents. He explained that it was emotionally difficult to watch his parents work long hours all for him, his brother, and their future.

I was interested and asked him how he expressed his love to his parents. He said they know he loves them. A Phlegmatic is not one to repeatedly tell someone of their affections. He shows them by the way he treats them and the gratitude he shows them. I got the impression that neither of his parents were a Phlegmatic and may need more affirmation. I suggested he begin communicating regularly with written notes. He would have time to think over the content while making them brief, to the point, but clearly expressing his love for them.

Respectfully submitted,
Eve J. Day, M.A.C.C.

12

Introducing The Sanguine

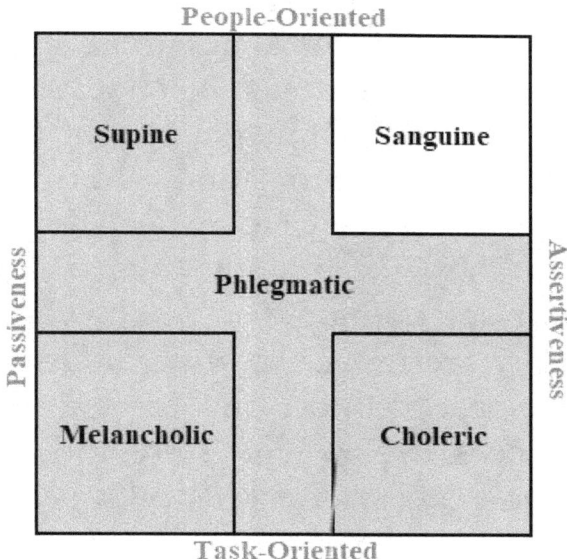

As we begin our discussion on the Sanguine, we will find that this temperament is perhaps one of the easiest to identify. As we begin, please remember that the strengths and weaknesses listed here are, as with the other temperaments, only tendencies. Each person will vary in intensity depending on where they are located within the grid. The closer anyone places to the outside corner increases their compulsion or intensity. The analysis done by a Temperament Therapist will determine where each person places on the grid.

Introduction

As we look at the diagram, we can make some general observations. Like the Choleric, the Sanguine is assertive, but they are much more interested in people than they are in tasks. When we say that they are assertive, we are saying they are out-going. They like people whether interacting with them or just being around them. They have a deep need for social interaction. They like brightly colored clothes and can be quite entertaining. People like being around them as they are fun to be with, amusing, have a positive up-beat attitude, and are encouraging to those who need it. You will rarely find a Sanguine alone by choice. They are either with people due to their own need or the fact that they naturally attract others who like being with them.

Their unique temperament adds a powerful dynamic to the mix. As we look at their tendencies, we will see the value they add as they make life a lot more fun and exciting.

General Tendencies of The Sanguine

The Sanguine is not only optimistic but has a high level of energy. They are enthusiastic about everything in which they are involved and bring a certain dynamic or life to any group or project. In their excitement, they tend to exaggerate certain facts because that is the way they see the final state or finished project. Everything is going to work out. Everything is going to be great and we are going to have so much fun. As long as we see the Sanguine from this perspective we realize that they are not intentionally misrepresenting the facts but rather expressing the possibilities.

To stay inspired, they relish their successes and want to celebrate with all who participated in the accomplishment. This is what motivates their drive. When it comes to their failures, they view them as momentary setbacks which, in the long run, will be inconsequential. A series of failures or setbacks can have its toll on them. However, to reignite their fire, all they need is to be with people.

The Sanguine is without a doubt the most popular of

the temperaments. They are wonderful motivators and encouragers. When working on tasks, they see that everyone has fun. If we stop for a moment and look at the preceding three temperaments we have examined so far, we can see how the addition of a Sanguine to the mix will help move things along with everyone enjoying the experience. Their temperament, like the others, was created by God Who understands the interactions and relationships necessary for humanity to thrive.

Strengths and Weaknesses of The Sanguine

Let's take a look at some of the strengths and weaknesses associated with the Sanguine. Because their energies are focused elsewhere compared to the others, they tend to lack some of the strengths that the other temperaments might take for granted. It is better for them if they partner with other temperaments. In their excitement and enthusiasm for life, they cast aside balance and caution. They tend to be drawn to people without regard to the activities in which these people are involved.

Sanguines need to find friends. They have a deep seated need to socialize even if the depth of those relationships are somewhat superficial. They are very likely to participate in the activities of the group without thinking about their morals, character, or behavior and without fully considering the consequences. When suggestions are made by the group for activities which go against their personal beliefs, the Sanguine will tend to go along with the group in order to be accepted. Although this can happen to any temperament, the Sanguine will most likely feel almost compelled to join in questionable activities especially during adolescence.

Emotions play an important part for the Sanguine in deciding what to do or how to do it. You can imagine the benefit of pairing them with other temperaments for stability. For example, the steadiness of the Phlegmatic or the thoroughness or detailed analysis of the Melancholic would provide them with a counterbalance. In exchange, they provide an optimistic and compassionate partner often meeting the needs of the more sober temperaments. When you look at examples like this, we can begin to understand the intricacy of God's Creation.

A Sanguine must stay busy and, if they don't, they can become stressed from the inactivity. Like the Supine temperament to follow, they both are people-oriented and, therefore, need human interaction like a plant needs sunshine. Quite often, as in the case of a pandemic when social distancing is necessary, the Sanguine and Supine can fulfill their needs for social interaction with the phone, live chat, and listening to talk shows.

Maintaining a positive attitude is important for the Sanguine. Frequently, they will cast-off rejection and negativity which causes them to reject the cautionary counsel of others. This has a lot to do with their child-like enthusiasm which makes them a great temperament with which to interact. All of us have weaknesses. Understanding our own weaknesses and those of others will allow us to learn to depend more upon the strengths of other temperaments.

13

An Example Of The Sanguine

The Sanguine scores high in the area of *Inclusion* for both expressed (their desire to interact with others) and wanted (their desire to have others interact with them.) They are social by nature and love people. They like the attention and communicating with others. They like spontaneity, love to have fun, and can be impulsive in their actions.

I met with Sarah who is 36 years old. She is a married female with two children. Her husband Steven is 40 years old and they have been married for 12 years. They were coming to counseling for issues in their marriage. It was evident that they loved each other very much and the husband would do anything to see her happy. However, their problem, at first, appeared to be financial.

Sarah was a salesperson for a medical supply distributor and was making great money until the pandemic. Sales dropped and so did her income. Steven is a Melancholic and worked as a financial analyst for an investment company. When they were flush with money, Sarah had always been able to spend money when she wanted. Steven was playing "the bad guy" and trying to manage their finances so they would not lose their home. The situation had become critical as they were now two months behind in their mortgage and the bank had sent them a letter. It was at this point they decided they needed someone to counsel them through this situation.

As we have already presented the Melancholic temperament, we will focus on the Sanguine temperament. You can probably imagine that Steve has the ability to handle the finances and already had a plan to get them out of this. Sarah had the problem. I asked if I could meet with Sarah alone for a while and bring Steve in towards the end of the sessions. I told them that this would allow Sarah to speak openly. They both agreed.

I began by explaining her temperament starting with the area of *Inclusion*. She was a Sanguine Compulsive. When we include the word Compulsive in the temperament title, it means that the tendencies for this area are much more extreme. I began by helping her understand her needs and then we would work to meet those needs in a constructive way. This would be best for both her and her family.

Speaking with her, she was outgoing, talkative, and I immediately felt we had established a friendship for communicating. In her sales career she visited her clients, had a great relationship with them, and the orders came rolling in. She placed top salesperson in her company several times. Completing tasks were not her "thing." Steve always took care of the tasks that needed to be done and they had a housekeeper who did the housework. However, that changed when they had to let the housekeeper go due to their finances. Now, without a job, the tasks of house-work, and not having the money to do with as she wanted, Sarah was very depressed and, perhaps, a little angry at God.

Her score in the area of *Control* was low in the ex-pressed and moderate in the wanted. So she was not looking to control others, but was willing to accept a moderate amount of control from others. This pro-vided hope for her allowing Steve to run the finances at least until they were back on their feet again.

We talked about God and the situation they found

themselves in. Bad things do not come from God, but sometimes He allows things to happen for a reason. Finding out what that reason is will be part of finding the solution. I had a pretty good idea what that was, but Sarah needed to find that out for herself. We prayed each time asking God to show her why He let this happen. I encourage all my clients to ask God why and I remind them to be looking for His answer.

Sanguines require connection with people. Lacking the people contact from her job she felt alone while at home doing house work. I recommended to put on a talk-radio program. Notice I didn't suggest the television. The talk-radio program would keep her engaged. Also, planning phone calls with friends or family at specific times and limiting them to allow for continuation of those conversations for another day. In other words, don't talk it all out. Save something to talk about tomorrow.

Sanguines are generally positive people and they need to maintain that positive outlook. After much discussion, Sarah agreed that Steve was the best suited to handle managing their finances. She trusted him and was confident in his ability. Sanguines can be compulsive shoppers when they are stressed or depressed. She gave Steve all her credit cards except a gas card. That solved one of their major causes of their debt. However, the depression still existed.

One of the blessings of a Sanguine is their spontaneity and their ability to make things fun. I told her there was no need for money to be the source of that fun. What she had plenty of was time. She needed to plan activities with the family and also alone with her husband. I challenged her creativity. We talked about a multitude of options: bike riding with the family, picnics with sandwiches in the park, and kayaking was a favorite activity with the family when they had time. Well, she needed to make time for the fun things with her family. I asked her what could she do to make a picnic alone with her husband romantic. She told me when they were first dating and both in college, they both had no money. Eating in the car at a drive-up hamburger stand was romantic. She got the idea and I could see her mind working on other ideas as well.

Understanding who she was, her needs, and how she could express who she was did help her. I followed up with a phone call about two months later. She couldn't talk long because Steve had saved enough money to take the family camping. She was happy. With his wife happy, this made Steve happy too. They were working through their challenges together. I asked her if she ever learned why God had allowed this to happen to them. She said she did. Now, life with her family has never been better.

Respectfully submitted,
Eve J. Day, M.A.C.C.

14

Introducing The Supine

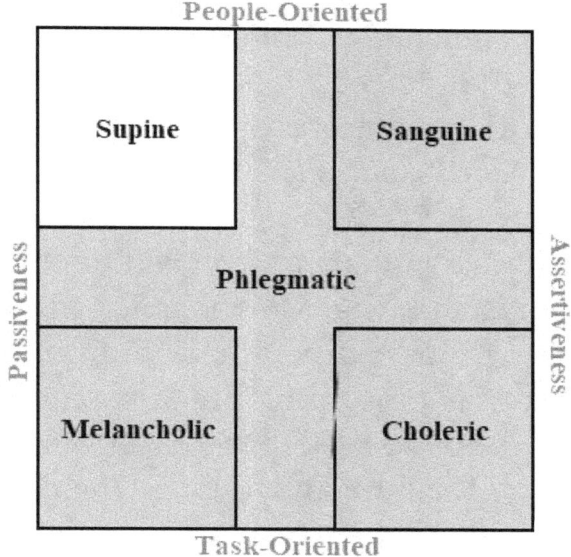

Identifying this particular temperament should be credited to Drs. Richard and Phyllis Arno. Their work brought to light the value and depth of the

Supine temperament. It is quite unique from the others. As we finish with this temperament, the last of the five, we make the reminder again: these are tendencies.

Introduction

A book written by two Christian authors, Ken Voges and Ron Braund, entitled *Understanding How Others Misunderstand You*[4] posits theories similar to those supported by the Drs. Arno. There is some difference in the nomenclature used. For example, instead of Choleric, Melancholic, Phlegmatic, and Sanguine, they use the terms Dominance, Compliance, Steadfast, and Influencer respectively. In neither this book nor *Spirit-Controlled Temperament*[5] by Tim LaHaye is the Supine temperament mentioned. Those attributes have been consolidated into either the Phlegmatic or the Melancholic. In other past studies, the Supine temperament did not exist. This area had not been identified as a separate temperament in addition to the other four until the research done by Drs. Richard and Phyllis Arno. It for this reason, we will include additional information for

---

[4] Ken Voges and Ron Braund, *Understanding How Others Misunderstand You–A Unique and Proven Plan for Strengthening Personal Relationship* (Chicago: Moody Press, 1995).

[5] Tim LaHaye, *Spirit-Controlled Temperament* (Tyndale: Carol Stream, Ill., 1993).

your consideration.

General Tendencies of The Supine

Supines are gentle souls with a servant's heart. They are most happy when they are serving others. Their life is a life of service sometimes without regard to their own personal needs. There is an example of the Supine in the Bible. In the following verses we are introduced to two sisters. We read in the Gospel of Luke 10:38-42:

> 38 Now it came to pass, as they went, that he entered into a certain village: and a certain woman named Martha received him into her house. 39 And she had a sister called Mary, which also sat at Jesus' feet, and heard his word. 40 But Martha was cumbered [overwhelmed] about much serving, and came to him, and said, Lord, dost thou not care that my sister hath left me to serve alone? bid her therefore that she help me. 41 And Jesus answered and said unto her, Martha, Martha, thou art careful [anxious] and troubled about many things: 42 But one thing is needful: and Mary hath chosen that good part, which shall not be taken

away from her.

Martha appears to be a stressed, task-oriented Choleric. However, her sister Mary is people-oriented. We find out that Mary is a Supine when we read in the Gospel of John 12:1-3:

> 1 Then Jesus six days before the passover came to Bethany, where Lazarus was which had been dead, whom he raised from the dead. 2 There they made him a supper; and Martha served: but Lazarus was one of them that sat at the table with him. 3 Then took Mary a pound of ointment of spikenard, very costly, and anointed the feet of Jesus, and wiped his feet with her hair: and the house was filled with the odour of the ointment.

To put this in context, this occurred the day before Jesus entered into Jerusalem on the day many call Palm Sunday. He is the promised Messiah. Mary anointed Him with oil. God used a Supine to fulfill this important service.

Strengths and Weaknesses of The Supine

Supines are often misunderstood as being weak and

indecisive. Since they are not task-driven, Cholerics may come to despise them as being worthless. This is far from being the case. They are the caretakers of the sick and elderly; those suffering or in pain from loss. Their selfless nature is gratified when those they help recover or are alleviated from suffering.

Their weakness is that they are vulnerable to misuse or even abuse. They have a high need for affection or appreciation, but they do not express that need to others. By hiding their emotions deep within, they make it difficult for others to understand them. They have an expectation that others will know their needs in the same manner as they know other's needs. They do not speak, act, or show any indication that they wish to be included in any social environment or relationship. This is due to their passive nature. They seek relationships with people as the Sanguine, but they make no sign or effort to achieve that. Unfortunately, Supines can be easily hurt.

When it comes to making decisions, they stall. Whether it is the lack of ability to analyze a situation or problem or the hesitation to act, they do better when they contribute to the decision process. They have a low expressed need for control and have little to no interest in controlling others. However, their wanted score is generally quite high. They want direction and follow direction from someone they trust willingly. They do not want to be dominated or unappreciated. When misused they internalize their anger. They find it hard, if not impossible, to confront anyone. Their inability to handle conflict often manifests itself in health issues.

The Supine requires love and affection. They crave appreciation or acknowledgment of their dedicated service. Without that, they will become depressed. They thrive in a relationship in which they feel loved and protected. In those situations, they are like a plant that flourishes with the right amount of water, nutrients, and sunlight. They prefer to react to the actions of others. This also applies to love and affection with their immediate family and close friends. They may rarely initiate, but they respond.

To summarize the Supine, they are the ones who serve with a loving heart. Their empathy is quite high. They feel the emotions of others and anticipate their needs. Their selfless service leaves them vulnerable to people who either intentionally or unintentionally do not appreciate the God-given value they bring to humanity.

15

An Example Of The Supine

The Supine is similar to the Sanguine as they are both people-oriented. However, the Sanguine is an extrovert and the Supine is an introvert. The former is quite likely to make the first move in a relationship while the latter will wait for the other person to initiate any interaction. When that happens, the Supine is more than eager to respond. We will see this become apparent in the following narrative.

Deborah prefers to be called Dr. Deb. She is 42 years old, a successful doctor of Ophthalmology which is the care for the eyes including surgery. She is also a mother of three active teenagers. I met with her several times with ongoing sessions as the need arises. The scores in both her *Inclusion* and *Control* areas confirm she is in the right profession as it requires a great amount of patience and high precision.

She decided to meet with me because she had been suffering from depression and a feeling of failure in her marriage. Her husband separated from her about a year before and is living the single lifestyle with little to no interaction with her or the children. Teenage years are difficult for any parent but especially challenging for a single parent who is juggling a profession.

We started our meetings by discussing her *Inclusion* score. You may recall we discussed a Melancholic Compulsive in a previous example. Deb's very low expressed score in *Inclusion* showed she had little to no interest in participating in social settings. Nor did she desire interaction from others. She was quite amiable when we met and showed no difficulty communicating or establishing a rapport.

Her temperament did not prevent her from making presentations before her medical colleagues. This she did on a regular basis as well as supervise interns. Public speaking was not something she wanted to do, but she did it out of necessity. I told her that she had the perfect temperament qualities for precision. If she were operating on a patient's eyes, how much social interaction would the patient want her to have during the course of the procedure? They would want her to be completely focused and not easily distracted.

Having reviewed the APS report before our meeting, I could see where the problem could be. When we got to the *Control* score, I needed to slow it way down. People need to feel confident that God made them and loves them. All of us need to understand our God-given temperament, accept it as a fact, and make accommodations to deal with it.

Part of any counseling process involves reading client's reactions. I rarely if ever counsel someone where we do not have a visual connection either in person or over a secure online meeting. I could tell she was getting very agitated as we moved into the area of *Control*. Her expressed score showed little to no interest in exercising control over others but a high desire to be controlled by others. Before we jump to the marriage, let's look at it from her profession. How much control concerning procedures, protocol, and medical knowledge would someone want their doctor to follow while operating on the eyes? The answer might be, "To the letter with no deviation, no creativity! Follow the rules!"

During several of our sessions we spoke specifically about her family history. She was a stellar student at any subject she studied. She attended medical school while working part-time to help support their young family. Once in medical school, she could no longer work. She took out student loans to support the family with the understanding that doctors will make a sufficient amount of money to pay back their student loans.

While her education took up several hours of the day, she still arranged to pick up and drop off the children at school, be part of their extracurricular activities, manage the house, and even cut the grass. The husband had a job but made sure he had a new pickup truck to transport himself to and from work. Every book starts with a blank page and, as she told her story, I begin to see a more complete picture.

She told me her husband hung on waiting for the big payday. However, there was the internship. Then came entry level positions at medical centers near her children's school. With the hectic and sometimes stressful home environment, she cared about stability for their children.

The husband's patience finally ran out. Now working full time, the large student loans needed to be repaid. There was a confrontation. She stated a fact: the student loans must be repaid. She quoted him as saying, "I have been patient long enough. I am leaving."

With that, he took his new truck and left. In spite of all this, he was still in control. At the urging of friends, she did seek legal advice which I will not discuss here.

Deb began to see the situation of her life clearer. Her husband appeared to be a Choleric perhaps even a Narcissist. She had become the door mat and he left for better opportunities. To help her with the children her mother came to live with them. She helps with the care of the home and transporting the children to their various schools. She did express that she would like companionship. Her score in *Affection* shows a moderate need to express her affection and a less moderate desire to receive it.

We discussed her need for affection and I suggested she take it slow. Pray about it. Ask God to send you someone when it is the right time for you. She needs to start by deciding where she wants the marriage to go. As this book is being written by two Temperament Therapists who are Christians, we do not feel the need or want the responsibility of judging anyone. The responsibility of judgment belongs to Christ alone. We can point them to various verses in the Bible for help and encouragement. However, we will support our clients' decisions whether we agree with it or not. That may separate us from some Christian counselors. In this Age of Grace, we do not teach God's judgment and condemnation. Rather, we proclaim His love and grace.

The Supine has a tendency to want someone else to tell them what they should do. For a therapist to do that would be creating a co-dependency. The number of sessions with Deb was more than normal, but in view of the situation, it was justifiable. It did come to a point where I knew she needed to move on and take control of her own life. I would have failed as a counselor not to teach her how to depend on God's leading. As Temperament Therapists, we teach who you are in Christ. You learn about all the many blessings and benefits there are by having a working relationship with Christ.

Now, Dr. Deb understood her temperament's strengths and weaknesses. She enjoyed a renewed relationship with her Lord. By depending on Christ, she would be able to make decisions as she continues to build faith and trust in Him.

Submitted by,
David A. Greene, Ph.D.

16

One Of A Kind

We are first introduced to colors in the primary grades like red, blue, green, yellow, and orange. We might learn that black is the absence of light and white is the presence of light. Our apologies to artists if we make this sound too simple. The point is when we learn something new, we are first introduced to it with its most basic structure or concepts. As art students progress, they learn to mix colors that can create unique masterpieces as they apply these colors to their canvas.

One of the biggest objections we receive when we teach temperament is that people do not want to be put in a box, stereotyped, or pigeon-holed. They will listen for only a short time, their mind having already been made up, put up their hand to signal "stop", and walk away. They are either someone who does not trust or someone whose mind is firmly set like concrete. This leads us to two important points. People are complicated. Not everything about someone's temperament is visible to the eye. Even a trained Temperament Therapist needs to use the APS temperament assessment tool to discover the part of the iceberg that lays beneath the surface.

We presented a basic introduction to the five temperaments. We summarized each of them individually and looked at the tendencies associated with each. The title of this chapter proposes that each of us is a masterpiece. Let us think about that for a moment. Rembrandt, Renoir, Michelangelo, da Vinci, van Gogh, Monet, Picasso, and Dalí are just a few examples of those who are honored with the name "the masters." They are known for their priceless creations of art. These "masters" created "masterpieces."

They did not exist before they were created. Their creation was not a random act out of chaos but rather done with thought and great attention to detail. They were created with intent. These masterpieces are each a product of the artist's creation. Each being unique even down to the choice of colors and signature brush strokes. We are the "masterpiece" who God created in His image according to the Bible. We are unique. We are one of a kind.

As His creation, we need to consider the concept of freewill. God gave each of us the freewill to make choices and to enjoy the benefits or suffer the consequences of the choices we make. There are tendencies within each temperament that may never be used. It is important to know that we exercise our freewill every time we make a choice. Someone who has a tendency towards explosive anger has the ability to choose to get angry or not; to channel that energy for good or bad. It is always a choice.

When we explain the strengths and weaknesses of different temperaments, we are often asked, "Why did God make so many different temperaments?" This is similar to asking, "Why did God use so many colors?" It is best explained by looking at the whole picture. A priceless masterpiece is best viewed from a relative distance. Its full value is not seen up too close. Likewise, the temperaments were designed to act together; to complement each other. Like colors in a painting, they are each part of the whole.

When we were born, we received the gift of life and our temperaments were instilled within us. Those temperaments have tendencies with strengths and weaknesses. Each of us needs to view our temperament as a gift. Our strengths are not only for our preservation, but they are to be used to serve others in their weaknesses and shortfalls. Picture members of a group interacting and working together for the common good. It is summed up in Christ's command in the Gospel of John 13:34:

> 34 A new commandment I give unto you,
> That ye love one another; as I have loved
> you, that ye also love one another.

In our present sinful state, we are fallen creatures. Designed by God in perfection, we tend to choose self and our own selfish ways.

Presently, sin with its desire to serve self is pervasive. Sin affects everything and everyone. How we use our temperaments will depend on our individual choice called freewill. In spite of sin, God chose people throughout the Bible with certain temperaments to achieve specific tasks. These people, although sinners, willingly chose to serve God.

Think about Moses. God gave the Law to Moses because of his temperament. He was able to slowly and accurately record God's Word. The Apostle Paul was given the task of bringing the Gospel of Grace to the Gentiles (*cf.* Gal. 2). God needed someone to carry a very important message without regard to numerous opponents. These are only two examples on how

God used sinful man to accomplish His objectives. Each of them had to choose, in spite of their weaknesses, to obey and serve God.

Let us consider the value of each temperament to a group or assembly. We will do this by looking at the various needs a group might have. The following scenario will help you see the value of each of the temperament within a group. Not only will it allow each to utilize their gifts, but it also serves to safeguard the group from their weaknesses.

There is the initial concept phase which handles the research and design. We will charge that to the Melancholic who is an abstract and creative thinker. This is followed by the checking, verification, supplies ordering, running it past the legal department, and other considerations. This will be entrusted to the Phlegmatic who will go over the design, point out any concerns, and make sure the plan is correct.

We will need someone to take charge of the implementation phase. This is someone who can direct the work, stay within the budget, and complete the project by the deadline. No one is better equipped to handle this than the Choleric. Their decisive action is valuable to the group as the Choleric moves the group along towards their ultimate goal.

Whether this is a volunteer project or not, the people doing the work are important. Someone needs to be there to motivate and encourage them to accomplish their collective activities. The people for that task would be the Sanguine. Few people have the gift to inspire and motivate people like the Sanguine. Like a proverbial cheerleader, they encourage everyone.

Finally, there is the care of the people. The Supine's task is to care for the people. They would arrange for food and drink, or possible emergency medical needs. In a perfect scenario, each temperament is working within each of their unique gifts. Together, everyone contributes to achieving the mutual goal.

Creation would be a beautiful place if each person considered others more valuable than themselves. We are speaking here about others collectively and not individually. Groups would function optimally with each need being met by someone uniquely created for that purpose. However, as you know, that is not the case. There always seems to be dissention amongst the members of any group. Many in the group put their own selfish needs or agendas ahead of the collective. When one component fails, the project could fail. We are telling you this so that you can see that you are valuable–your unique contribution is appreciated.

So, what can we do when there are interpersonal problems? This question can be applied to any group: families, volunteer groups, churches, and places of employment. Temperament Therapy is specifically designed to address this issue. Unlike secular counseling, Temperament Therapy begins by teaching. They teach people who they are–who they were created to be. That is easily expanded to include others with whom there is conflict.

Reconciliation and healing come through understanding. Our understanding can begin by each of us asking the question, "How am I wired?"

17

Temperament Therapy

Temperament Therapy is different. We have presented the five temperaments with examples of individuals. You can see how God made all the pieces of humanity fit together like a beautiful mosaic. Each person is unique with every person having a connection to their Creator whether they acknowledge it or not. Denying something exists does not make it not true. Each of us was created or designed to have a relationship with our Creator. That choice is ours to make.

As Faith-based Counselors, we start by acknowledging the fundamental truth that God is our Creator. We are all wired by Him to form our own unique temperament. Like the expensive watch with all its intricate and detailed workmanship, we are not the product of random chaos. Our intricate physical, mental, and emotional designs are uniquely made. Again, we are not the result of a long process of evolution starting from nothing. Anyone who studies systems of any sort will agree that order cannot be the product of random chaos. Where there is a design, there *is* also a Designer.

We started with that for a reason. It is what makes Temperament Therapy different from other forms of counseling. The average length of temperament counseling is under 10 sessions. On-going support and encouragement can continue with the therapist. Our goals include helping the client know who they were created to be. We want them to develop their relationship with their Creator. We should all be on a first name basis with Him.

The Temperament Therapist works as a helper, supporter, teacher, brother or sister in Christ, and, most importantly, an encourager. As ordained ministers our role is to introduce you to Christ, if you do not know Him, and help you establish a relationship with Him as your Friend and Counselor. In the Bible, the title of God's Holy Spirit is "the Comforter." (See Jn. 14:16, 26; 15:26; 16:7.) In these verses, He is also referred to as "the Spirit of Truth." We want to encourage everyone who wants to come to the knowledge of truth to seek Him in His Word–the Bible.

As you can see from the examples provided, much of our counseling time is spent teaching. It is important to understand that we will not take on the role of judging our clients. We point out dangers such as excessive drinking may cause personal injury and could endanger others. The only obligation we have as counselors is to inform the appropriate authorities in the event of a crime or a clear and present danger to someone including the client. That is both our legal and moral obligation.

Most of the examples we gave show the client being the central part of the therapy. The scope of Temperament Therapy goes beyond individuals. With a couple, both complete the APS assessment. Then, we focus on each individual and their strengths and weaknesses as they interrelate. This can also apply to extended family and even co-workers. Ultimately, it comes down to this: who did God create each of us to be? What is our unique temperament? How does our unique temperament compilation act, think, and feel? How does it interact with others? Like we said before, we start with the APS and then start coloring in the picture until the clients can see a picture of themselves clearly. Helping God to achieve that in each client's life is the best feeling in the world!

Both of us hope that this was an exciting introduction

to the many blessings we have from God when we understand who He made us to be.

May God richly bless you.

Eve J. Day, M.A.C.C.
and David Alan Greene, Ph.D.

Resource

National Christian Counselors Association
640 Apex Road
Sarasota, FL 34240

Phone: 941-388-6868
Website: ncca@ncca.org

Other GraceWord Publications

Complete Surveys Of The Bible:

Letters To Theophilus
The Glorious Destiny Of Israel
The Hidden Gospel: Once Hidden But Now Reveal.

Expositional Commentaries Of The Bible:

1st Corinthians: Dispensationally Considered
1st & 2nd Thessalonians: Disp. Considered
1st & 2nd Timothy & Titus: Disp. Considered
2nd Corinthians: Dispensationally Considered
Acts: Dispensationally Considered
Colossians & Philemon: Disp. Considered
Ephesians: Dispensationally Considered
Galatians: Dispensationally Considered
Hebrews: Dispensationally Considered
Philippians: Dispensationally Considered
Revelation: Dispensationally Considered
Romans: Dispensationally Considered

The Gospel of John: Dispensationally Considered
The Gospel of Luke: Dispensationally Considered
The Gospel of Mark: Dispensationally Considered
The Gospel of Matthew: Disp. Considered
The Seven Hebrew Epistles: Disp. Considered

Other Books

How Am I Wired?
Two Distinct Gospel Messages Of The N.T.

About The Authors

David Alan Greene, Ph.D. received his Bachelor of Theology, Master of Biblical Studies, and Ph.D. in Biblical Studies from Evangelical Theological Seminary. He continued his studies and obtained a Ph.D. in Christian Counseling through the National Christian Counselors Association. He has written numerous books, is an evangelist, and teaches the Bible rightly divided. He uses temperament analysis to adapt his teaching to individuals.

Eve J. Day, M.A.C.C. received her Bachelor of Christian Counseling from Evangelical Theological Seminary and her Master of Clinical Christian Counseling through the National Christian Counselors Association. As a faith-based Christian counselor, she uses temperament therapy to specialize in family and children counseling.

www.ingramcontent.com/pod-product-compliance
Lightning Source LLC
Chambersburg PA
CBHW071757120626
46550CB00002B/831